INDIAN ARTIFACTS

VIRGIL Y. RUSSELL

Author

1895 - 1957

INDIAN ARTIFACTS

VIRGIL Y. RUSSELL
A. B and M. A.
1927-1957
Head of the Social Science Department
Natrona County High School
Casper, Wyoming

With Pen Sketches by

STELLA L. RUSSELL

First Printing
1951
1000 copies

Second Printing
1953
2000 copies

Third Printing—Revised
1957
5000 copies

Fourth Printing
1962
5000 copies

Fifth Printing
1966
5000 copies

Sixth Printing
1970
5000 copies

Seventh Printing
1974
5000 copies

Published and sold by Mrs. Virgil Y. Russell
1342 South Poplar, Casper, Wyoming

Printed by Johnson Publishing Company
Boulder, Colorado
1962

Dedicated to my devoted, hard working, helpful, and capable wife, Stella. If this book is of any value to collectors, they owe a debt of gratitude to her for it was her continual "prodding" that made me put my meager knowledge of artifacts onto the printed page. She loves this book, has more faith in it and has put more hours into its production than I or anyone else.

PREFACE

I wrote INDIAN ARTIFACTS OF THE ROCKIES as a venture. I am grateful for the splendid reception it received. Now, as I am preparing a revised and enlarged third printing of my second book, INDIAN ARTIFACTS, I feel indebted to the many collectors from coast to coast who have accepted my efforts to prepare a book for amateurs in such a responsive way.

I wish to repeat that INDIAN ARTIFACTS is written primarily for the amateur collector of Indian artifacts. Before writing my first book I made intensive investigation and found very little material in books or manuals that would be of assistance to the amateur collector in hunting, identifying, arranging, displaying, and preserving Indian artifacts. I find these conditions virtually unchanged today. And so, because of the apparent need of amateur collectors and the pressure brought upon me by my wife and son, I again prepare to "go to press".

I was not able to classify all of the artifacts found in the Rocky Mountain region in my first book; neither am I able to describe and classify all of the artifacts found in the United States in this one. I have added artifacts and revised material in this third printing, and have tried to present information on a great many different artifacts found in this country. Again, I caution the reader not to forget that I am one of the first to admit that I do not describe and classify *all* of the artifacts found in the United States in this treatise. In addition to research in books, I have written to many of the outstanding collectors of our country and have received much information from them.

I have not attempted to add any scientific information to the material already presented by scholars, but I am trying to write and speak in terms that the average collector, from

Boy Scout to adult, who has a few specimens, will understand and thereby gain information and assistance in starting, identifying or caring for his collection. Later, he will *graduate* from this volume and be ready to study the works of outstanding archaeologists. I still recall my efforts to secure information when I started collecting, and realize what a help a book of this kind would have been to me. Thus I am willing to attempt, once again, to prepare manuscript.

I have been speaking in the first person, but I must not neglect to say that all of the drawings were made by my wife, Stella. I will have to confess that many of the compliments received on the book in the past were based on the fine drawings which she sketched. All drawings in which artifacts are identified as belonging to various collectors, are exact reproductions of the artifact, flake for flake. My wife decided to sketch many of the artifacts because workmanship on many fine specimens is often not revealed in photographs.

I wish also to express gratitude to my hundreds of students who continue to bring me pieces and ask, "What is this?" This and other questions keep me busy and make me continue to search for more information which will be of assistance to amateur collectors.

VIRGIL Y. RUSSELL

Virgil passed away May 6, 1957 but I believe he left a rich heritage to all people interested in preserving these relics of our first Americans and I will continue to print the books as long as the demand warrants.

MRS. VIRGIL Y. RUSSELL

1342 S. Poplar
Casper, Wyoming 82601

INTRODUCTION

THERE are hundreds of different kinds of collectors in our country. They collect coins, stamps, guns, antiques, buttons, autographs, or anything from fire engines to miniatures of all kinds. It can almost be stated that every man is a collector whether he realizes it or not. Of this great array of collectors, it is doubtful if there are any more avid or enthusiastic than those who hunt, buy and collect the artifacts of our primitive man, popularly called Indians, but known to scholars as "Amerinds" as distinguished from the people of India.

At some time Indians made their homes in or they traversed every state in the Union. Their remains, relics and stone artifacts are found in caves or mounds, sandblows, on the surface, in graves, excavations or almost anywhere. It is said of gold, "Gold is where you find it." The same is true of the Indian's artifacts. We used to say of the Indian, "Where you don't think there is an Indian, that is where you will find him." The same often applies to his artifacts. You may look carefully and find none; a few minutes later a companion may come along and find a beautiful specimen. No wonder some people used to say "they rained down."

It is true that commercialism has injured this fascinating hobby. Such high prices are paid for good artifacts that it removes many of the best specimens from the reach of the majority. However, that is true of almost any hobby. It is doubtful if any major hobby is less commercialized. One will find many collectors who absolutely refuse to sell their specimens. Recently a collector who had a fine Yuma refused to sell it but *gave* it to the Yuma collector to be displayed in his Yuma collection.

Another criticism sometimes voiced is that there are "fakes" turned out by white men. This is true, but it is also true of other items which are collected. Even United States coins are counterfeited. But it is difficult to deceive an old time collector, for he can identify the "fakes" as easily as a diamond collector can distinguish a diamond from a piece of glass.

The majority of the countries of the world have some type of stone relic made by their primitive man. However, they all differ from our Indian stone work, even though there is a similarity in all stone workmanship, regardless of where it is found. Nevertheless, those of Egypt and Denmark, for instance, can come close to equalling in excellence and quality of workmanship some of our artifacts. Few countries have the great quantity of artifacts which are found in the United States.

There may be small towns that do not have a collector of Indian artifacts, though it is doubtful. Someone in that little village probably has an arrow, spear, or stone implement, if not a large collection.

The majority of towns and cities have small or large museums. The stone artifacts usually gravitate to a museum, be it small or large. Some curators of museums are so short sighted that they resent the fact that some collectors "buy" specimens, thus preventing museums from obtaining them. They err in this lack of foresight. The collector who purchases material gathers together the stray specimens into a collection. Eventually, his collection will be inherited by an heir who does not want them. Then they will be donated to a museum, as a monument to the old collector. Everyone will benefit by the collector's efforts and money. He hunted, purchased and gathered together a collection of strays that otherwise would have been lost! Hats off to the tireless efforts of this pioneer who did not wait around to have specimens given to him, but went out and secured them, by hook or crook, by sweat or dollar, letting nothing stand in his way.

THAT YOU MAY KNOW

THIS book is written for the amateur collector and not for the advanced scholar of archaeology.

I do not claim to have identified or illustrated all of the stone artifacts of the Indian, but I have identified the majority of the more common ones—over ninety—in this small volume.

This book contains pictures of collections. I have not viewed or studied all of these many speciments so that I cannot vouch for every artifact as being authentic or what it is claimed to be; I only print the owners identification. However, I do vouch for the ones that I use to identify a specific artifact.

I cannot answer all of the letters concerning the identification or authenticity of various artifacts. Drawings are often misleading and one has to see, study and handle the stone artifacts in order to answer authoritatively. Lately my mail has become so heavy that I find it impossible to reply to all. Each book is probably read by at least ten people during the life of the book and that would mean some 40,000 people. It isn't that I am unappreciative or want to be rude, but I do not have a secretary and to reply to all who write, has become an impossibility. Practically every collector has at least one artifact that stumps him and he wants to stump me. He usually does. Many of these stone artifacts are general purpose tools and some were used for skills and techniques that are no longer used in our present civilization. Thus, I do not believe that any living person can tell what all tools were used for or all of the uses of many tools. However, throughout the book and in the Chapter on ACKNOWLEDGMENTS, I have often furnished names and addresses of authorities on various subjects. They are often glad to answer questions.

I now have the finest Yuma collection in existence; I am always anxious to add to it. Some collectors want their Yumas in my collection so that they will always be preserved and kept in this outstanding collection and have graciously donated their fine specimens. I will promise to never sell them out of the collection and always will use the name of the owner to identify the artifacts unless he prefers otherwise. However, I will pay what I feel I can afford for a good Yuma to add to my collection, providing there is a complete history of the specimen to accompany it.

TABLE OF CONTENTS

Part I

ACQUIRING A COLLECTION

Part II

INDIAN ARTIFACTS IDENTIFIED

VIRGIL, JR.

The scholar and the one who values artifacts for their educational value. Every piece and specimen is "priceless" to him and must be preserved and kept for posterity.

PART ONE

ACQUIRING A COLLECTION

CHAPTER 1

HOW TO START A COLLECTION

THERE are various ways to start your artifact collection, but the one most generally used is to go out and hunt for it. This is the slow hard way, but it is the one that entwines your affections around each piece. Every piece has pleasant and happy recollections. You study each piece and the knowledge gained remains with you. The exercise and fresh air you get while hunting is worth untold dollars to you, both physically and mentally. You can always find kindred souls who will willingly go with you and the friendship built in this way is lasting. Keep a record of every piece—where it was found, when and in connection with what bones or other artifacts. If possible, make a drawing of each piece to catalogue with the other information.

Another method is to buy a collection. There are times when you find collectors who have grown tired of their artifacts, who are moving away and cannot take their collection with them, or for some other reason are willing to sell their collection. Buy this collection and use it as a nucleus for your own or if you have one, add it to yours. This is a duty as well as a business proposition. The precious artifacts must not be lost. Get the owner's record of each piece and file it away. If he has found his artifacts, he can usually tell you where each piece was found.

Another way to build a collection is to trade with other collectors. There are many collectors who will trade pieces but will not sell. Check magazines for names; there are many in your part of the country who will exchange.

Then there is the professional dealer who will sell to you. I may add that genuine artifacts are getting increasingly scarce and difficult for dealers to obtain for resale and more and more they are taking the attitude of "let the buyer beware." One prominent dealer even has the following printed on his letterhead: "I sell all relics or material subject to buyers inspection, judgment and approval. I guarantee nothing to be prehistoric, new or old or any age."

There is always the medium of the advertising column of the various magazines for collectors. A small ad stating what you want will often bring very good results, but do not do this until you know your artifacts and can tell a "fake" from a genuine piece.

There are three types of artifacts. One glance will reveal the genuine type; they show traces of patina, sand scratches and old age. Then there are the questionable ones, difficult to tell. Lastly, the one that is so freshly made it shines in your eyes. Send both of these latter types back. Do not keep the doubtful ones. Purchase only of people who will send you pieces for inspection. The majority of collectors are very willing to send pieces for inspection for either trade or sale with the understanding: "both parties satisfied or no deal."

The last method which I will direct attention to is that of "hunting collections." Pick out that part of the country that has the type of artifact you desire to collect. Go to the Chamber of Commerce, filling stations, general grocery stores, or the post office, and ask, "Who has a collection of Indian artifacts in this town?" The answer is practically always forthcoming. Then, when you meet this collector, he usually knows all fellow collectors in that locality, and your contacts are made. Have your trading material with you. Bring artifacts found in your home locality; he is often glad to trade his local material for yours. This will benefit

A part of the well displayed collection containing thousands of artifacts gathered and mounted by the late Louis Brunke of Colorado Springs, Colorado. Now owned by his wife.

Attractive, historical fireplace of William Hutton, Jr., Green River, Wyoming.

both of you. I personally have met hundreds of collectors in this way and have never met a disagreeable one.

In the winter, when one has the most time to pursue a hobby, it is impossible to go out and hunt artifacts as the ground is covered with snow. The objection may be removed by hunting "by the fireside." During the winter of 1949, records were broken all over the country in sub-zero temperatures, depth of snow and blizzards of long duration which blocked trains and stalled all transportation for days. However, during that severe winter, a few collectors did more real hunting than they had for years. The weather was too severe to get out and work or enjoy outdoor relaxation, so these intrepid collectors devised a new way of hunting artifacts.

They needed a comfortable chair, a warm room, a desk, writing paper and maps. Stamps took the place of gasoline. They first selected the portion of the country in which they wished to hunt, then studied a map of this territory. If the territory included a large city, letters were sent to the Chamber of Commerce asking for names of collectors. If the towns were smaller, queries were mailed to the postmaster. Rural areas were contacted by writing letters to the school teachers of the country schools. The letters to the teachers were usually accompanied by drawings and sketches describing what the collectors wanted and suggesting prices they might pay. This helped the children to know what was wanted and the word "pay" did much to encourage them to go through their old tin cans, cigar boxes, and trinkets, and pick out specimens in which they had long ago lost interest. Many adult collectors contacted often would not sell but were glad to trade artifacts.

Each collector contacted in this manner knew other collectors, both locally and in other parts of the country, and contacts grew by leaps and bounds.

This method enables an Indian artifact collector to hunt,

Fractured base type of arrowheads and spears. All of those pictured were surface finds from Ohio, although this type of point is also found in Indiana and Kentucky. The fractured part of the base has been ground after fracturing. From the collection of Mack Schumm of Circleville, Ohio, who specializes in this type of point.

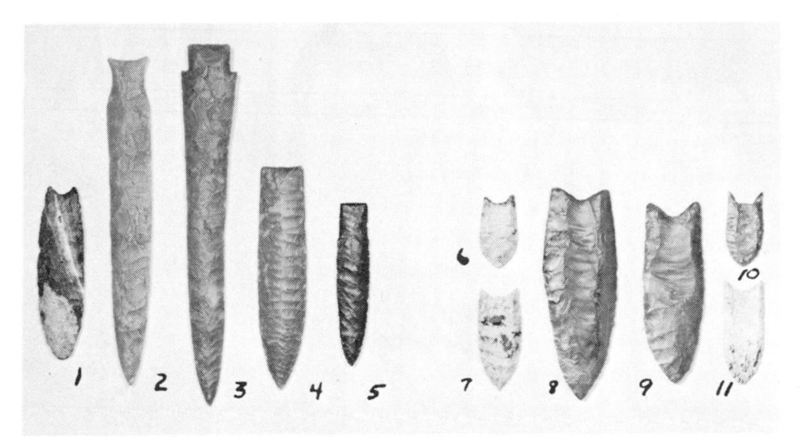

A few of the very fine specimens of the collection of the Rev. S. P. Martz, Shamokin, Pennsylvania, who identifies them as follows: Yumas —1, from Brown's End, Colorado; 2 and 3, Jefferson County, Missouri; 4, found in the Rio Grande River, Big Bend area of Texas; 5, Dallas County, Texas; Folsoms—6, found at Clovis, New Mexico; 7, Calico Rock, Arkansas; 8, Simpson County, Kentucky; 9, Marshall County, Kentucky; 10 and 11, Union County, New Mexico.

not only in summer, but in all kinds of weather and to collect many worth-while friends as well as specimens. As his collection grows, so do his acquaintances and a bond of friendship is formed that binds the collectors together. Few hobby bonds are stronger than that of the Indian artifact collectors.

It is possible to use this method to hunt in all foreign lands, for while it is true they had no Indians, nevertheless, they did have their stone age periods. Many of their stone age specimens closely resemble the stone work of the American Indian and therefore make splendid additions to a collection.

You may devise methods of gathering a collection other than those discussed here. Do not forget that collections are really built on interest, love of artifacts, and persistence.

CHAPTER 2

DECIDING ON TYPE OF COLLECTION

IT is well to give a little time and thought as to what kind of Indian artifacts you desire to collect.

The most common type is that in which the collector keeps everything he finds, from complete pieces to the smallest chips. The only essential label on it is, "I found it." This will probably meet the demands of the majority of collectors. There are other collectors who try to secure some stone artifacts from every state in the Union, even branching out into foreign countries. One collector has the outline of a large map burned into buckskin. The stone artifact is fastened onto the state from which it was obtained. This makes a very picturesque display.

There are many collectors who try to obtain a representative piece of all artifacts—from the smallest bird point to the largest spear. They work on number of kinds and types of artifacts. This type of collection is very educational. This collector will trade any of his duplicates for some piece he does not have.

Then there are those who go in for the unusual pieces, or specialize in collecting one particular type of artifact. There are at least two collectors who have concentrated on Yuma points. One of these spent more than twenty years in searching, hunting and digging. The other spent years in hunting collections and picking out the Yumas—usually about one Yuma in twenty collections.

There is the collector who picks out a certain site. He digs, sifts, and gets everything down to the smallest fragment from this one site. Other pieces have no value to him. One of the largest collections in Wyoming is one which contains several thousand bird points. This collector takes great pride in his many colors, shapes, and materials.

There is a collector who is interested only in Yumas and Folsoms. He has more than four hundred Folsoms, many of which he obtained from people who picked them up during the "great black blizzard" in southeastern Colorado and western Kansas. There are those who collect their artifacts according to tribes.

It matters little what you collect. It is the love of the open, the fresh air, the exercise, the thrill of getting away from the "maddening crowd," the feeling that you are discovering and saving something for posterity. Check over the suggestions made in this chapter. Possibly, some of them will cause you to exclaim, "Ah, here is the type of collection I want!" On the other hand, perhaps none of these suggestions will suit your interests, but in considering them you may stumble upon an idea as to just what you want in a collection.

Collectors frequently find artifacts that appear to be unfinished. This is especially true of various knives and scrapers. They appear to be imperfect artifacts but when examined carefully the *imperfections* are actually hand or finger holds, made to keep the hand from slipping when the tool became greasy or bloody while being used, and to enable the user to grasp it more firmly at all times.

Study the artifact carefuly, handle it several different ways and see if the fingers or thumb will fit into the indentations on the tool. Sometimes it fits the right hand and sometimes the left. Many artifacts reveal that a large number of Indians used their tools in the left hand. Their hand tools were expertly made and fit the hand well.

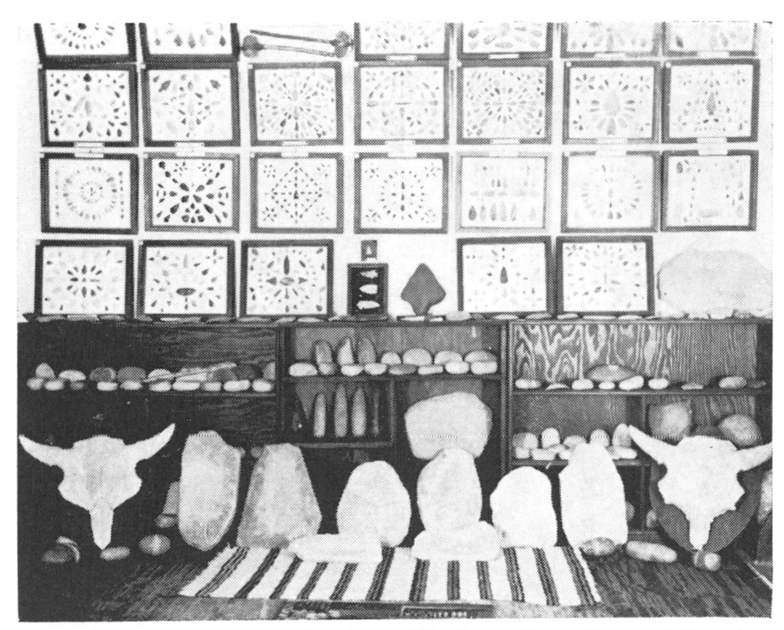

The "I found it myself" collection of E. C. Swallow, Casper, Wyoming. There are many fine collections in Wyoming, but few, if any, which have been gathered by the efforts of one man, excell Mr. Swallow's collection. Mr. Swallow prides himself and justly so, not only on the quality of his collection but also on the fact that he found them himself.

Individually framed spears, hung on Navajo blanket. Center piece is 6½ inches long. Walter Jones collection.

Beautiful bannerstones. Center one is 6½ inches long. Wm. Smail collection, Loogootee, Illinois.

CHAPTER 3

SUGGESTIONS FOR HUNTING ARTIFACTS

THE main essential in hunting artifacts is the ambition and the desire to get out and just hunt; however, in this chapter, I will mention several things that may be helpful and of value to you.

First, it is a big help to have a car to get away from the main highways—away to where the land is inhabited by game and practically uninhabited by modern man. A car will help in getting you far away. Take a shovel along and a few other tools so that if you get stuck you can dig out. A pair of wire stretchers can prove helpful in getting a car out of a mudhole; drive down a stake, attach the wire stretcher to the car and the stake, and you can thus give a good many pounds of pull, helping to get the car moving again.

Plenty of water and a canteen always come in handy. There is no pleasure in hunting if you are "dying of thirst." Take along a broom handle or round stick, into one end of which a nail has been driven, leaving the head of the nail protrude. This tool will enable you to flick out any prospective piece which is sighted. Usually it is just a rock; but it is necessary to check every suspicious looking stone. This methods saves one from bending over again and again, and saves many a backache. Don't forget the food and plenty of it. Food tastes mighty good after hours of tramping over the hills, rocks and through the sand blows.

If you are a Mr. Cautious, take along first aid for snake bite. I don't think I ever heard of anyone being bitten by a rattler while hunting arrow heads, but it could happen. It is just as well to wear hiking boots or leather leggings as few people are even bitten above the knee. The reptile usually strikes the foot, ankle or some place below the knee.

Matches and a pocket knife may come in handy. A compass is not necessary, but if one is owned it can be used to help find your way back to the car at the end of a long day's search.

There are probably as many different methods of hunting for artifacts as there are collectors. Each has his own "pet" method. The ones given here are ones told to me by various collectors. Each method has some one who will say it is the best.

Many collectors hunt for sand blows and blow outs. Many people prefer to go out just after a hard rain or wind storm. They consider the side from which the wind usually blows to be the better location. Here the wind usually blows from the southwest, moving the sand to the northeast. Thus the southwestern part of a blow would be the better place to look because the artifact would be covered up on the northeastern side.

There are those who look for buffalo traps. These are sheer cliffs dropping down from a long level surface of prairie. The Indians chased the buffalo over the prairies at great speed, headed them for the cliff; when they reached the edge, they could not turn back and those in the rear pushed them over. The Indians then went to the foot of the cliff and killed the wounded buffalo with their stone implements. It was impossible to drag the heavy carcass very far, so the bones and artifacts are found at the foot of these cliffs where they were used. Weathering, wind, freezing, rain and erosion have caused portions of these cliffs to fall down and cover up the remains, but many collectors find their arti-

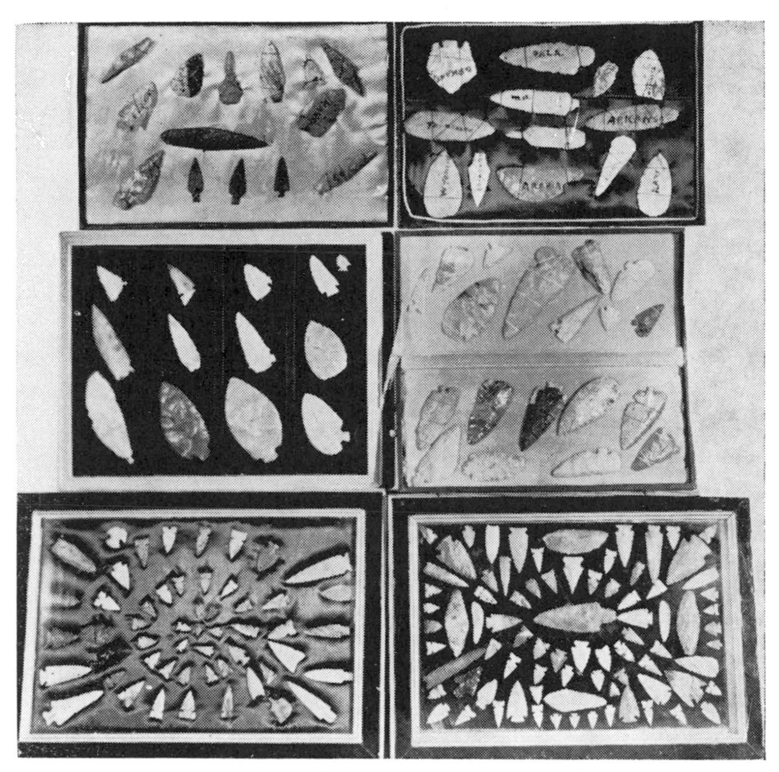

Mr. R. B. Ravenscroft of Liberal, Kansas owns one of the largest tang knife collections ever gathered. Two frames of tang knives and scrapers are pictured. Mr. Ravenscroft's collection is one of the best known and most widely publicized in Western Kansas. Mr. Ravenscroft is an ardent collector of Indian artifacts.

facts at the foot of these cliffs by digging and removing this weathered material.

Some collectors search for Indian graves and dig up the remains. They find beads and ornaments and some even take the skeletons. The graves are usually hard to locate. Piled boulders that give evidence of being placed by hand denote a grave beneath, unless a sheep herder may have been in the vicinity and piled them in his spare time and then they are known as "sheep herder's monuments." Beads in an ant hill often betray a grave beneath or in the vicinty. There are states that have laws against molesting graves of any kind. It is just as well not to resort to this method of collecting.

There are those who, when searching on sandy places, get down on their hands and knees and crawl. This method is slow and tedious (and hard on the knees!) but often brings results. Frequently just a small portion of the artifact shows above the surface and one may find it when crawling along. Many artifacts have been found in plowed fields.

Some say that they always walk with the sun to their backs and watch for color, trusting to the sun to reflect the color of the stone. They seem to know the best time of day when the sun is at the right angle to give the best reflection.

Still others say they prefer to hunt back from a water hole about one-quarter to one-half of a mile. The Indian usually hid near the water hole and shot his arrow at the game while it was drinking. This did not ordinarily bring instant death and the animal usually ran about one-quarter to one-half of a mile before falling.

Hunting for artifacts can be done in various ways as I have suggested. If you are one who is gathering your collection the hard way, by digging for it, you will probably appreciate the following account of a couple who dig for their relics.

In the fall of 1956 it was my pleasure to become acquainted with two of the most "dedicated" relic collectors I have ever met. Their complete dedication to their work is as refreshing as a cooling shower in mid-summer. I will include an account of their relic digging at the Mandan site, but first I want to introduce my readers to Mr. and Mrs. M. P. Mosbrucker by means of a few questions and answers.

When did you become interested in the Mandan Indian relics?

"I started digging for Mandan Indian relics back in 1913 and through the years of 1913 to 1916 I worked at different times with Mr: Steinbruck who was seeking relics for the North Dakota Historical Society. Then I went to war and home again in late 1919. In the spring of 1920 I did a little surface hunting. I continued on through 1926 when I married a woman who was also much interested in Indian relics, so we made that our hobby and spent all of the time possible afield, gathering a couple of nice collections consisting mostly of arrow points, scrapers and heavy stone implements. The collections were partially broken up and given to different museums and we helped one collector complete his collection. Surface hunting was very fruitful and easy during the blow years of the 30's. We started digging in the Boley site in July of 1952 and the thrill of digging into the soil and finding beautiful Indian relics possessed us and to date we are still doing it. One never knows what they are going to come up with, seldom a day passes but that something odd and new shows up."

How deep did you dig?

"The outer edges were worked to a depth of from three to four feet, the larger portion of the central part worked to bedrock or clay bottom which was fourteen feet deep. Test holes were dug which showed artifacts and ash layers to that depth."

How many artifacts have you obtained?

"Up until the close of 1955, over 70,000 items were taken from the sites worked in this village."

What was your greatest thrill?

"That's a tough question. The whole job was packed with thrills; every day we spent digging brought a thrill. It is hard to say which was the greatest—whether it was finding a 3¾ pound celt made of beautiful black rock, shaped to perfection or long slender bone needles, nice bone awls, bone fishhooks, pierced elks teeth or beautiful arrowheads. In fact, when you know that you are doing something that you love to do the thrill is there regardless of what it is you come up with."

Have there been any interesting sidelights during your digging?

"There are just too many to enumerate. Just imagine two people spending four years shoveling dirt, doing something that no amount of money could entice them to do! There must have been something there of interest or they would not have kept that up day after day, for four years, never tiring of the job, never complaining, sometimes in near freezing weather and sometimes when it was a hundred above in the shade and no shade available. We never had a moments regret for all of the backaches we have had."

How many work hours would you estimate you have put in?

"That too is a question that is hard to answer. The hours did not count for it was not being done for pay; you might say it was a labor of love. But we were out there every day that the weather did not keep us from being there, during the summer months when I was not working at my regular job, the wife and I would go out there around six in the morning and with a light lunch along, we would stay until dark. For four consecutive years we spent our entire vacations out there every day. During work days, I worked at my job until three P.M. daily and then came home and we went out until dark. In 1952-53, the winter did not set in until January 5th, 1953 at three P.M. when snow drove us back to town. How many hours? That's hard to say, but they were happy ones!"

One last question, What do you expect to do with your vast, priceless collection?

"That is a question I have considered many times. At the present time we are displaying and lecturing on the artifacts of the Mandan Indians, trying to follow up the culture, habits and lives of the Indians. We feel that these artifacts should never leave North Dakota. So, either they will be given to the North Dakota Historical Society, or if Morton County (in which they were found) erects a museum, the artifacts will be installed there."

And now, in Mr. Mosbruckers own words, his account of the Mandan Indian and his relics.

THE MANDAN INDIANS AND THEIR ARTIFACTS

M. P. Mosbrucker,
Mandan, North Dakota

This report on the Boley site, MO 37, represents just the work of two people, Mr. and Mrs. M. P. Mosbrucker of Mandan, North Dakota, who have gone into it as a part of their hobby of collecting relics of the Mandan Indians. At the time this adventure was first undertaken, we had no idea of what we were running into or what the outcome would be. We had known of the site for many years and had done quite a bit of surface hunting througout the whole village and the results of such hunting had been surprising through the years.

The site is located five miles north of the city of Mandan, North Dakota and is the site of a known Indian village, formerly occupied by the Mandan Indians and abandoned by them about the time of the smallpox epidemic circa 1764. There is no record of the village being occupied thereafter. No contact material has been found during the exploration of the mounds by the Mosbruckers. One Catholic medal was found at the three foot level, which could not have been older than around three hundred years for had it been the inscription thereon would no doubt have been in Spanish, it was in English. Some research has been done on this medal but nothing definite has come up as yet.

The Boley site is one of the many Mandan Indian village sites along the Missouri River in North Dakota. It was named the Boley site after the owner, Mr. Boley, who filed it as a homestead in the early days. Like the majority of these sites it lies on the higher terrace along the Missouri River, some few sites have been known to lie on the bottom land proper. The site is high and well above the spring flood level, ice packs have not been known to ever reach the terrace. The entire village lies on an area which has very little slope, just enough to create a fair runoff of water towards the southeast. It extends right to the edge of a high bank of the Missouri which at one time no doubt flowed at the base of the terrace; now the Missouri has changed its course and there is quite a bit of "made land" between the terrace and the banks of the river.

The Boley site, at the center of Section 33, Township 140, Range 81, covers between eight and ten acres and lies at the junction of a small creek and the Missouri River. The greater portion of the site has been under cultivation for a long number of years, and in 1909 it was cut through by the railroad. A few cache pits show in the railroad cut, and many lodge pits show very plainly in portions of the field. Seven refuse heaps were at the edge of the terrace on the east side and one bordering the small creek on the north end.

In 1950 work was started on the two refuse heaps on the

southeast end of the village, the largest of these being 32′ x 66′ and the smaller 20′ x 24′. The larger of the two proved very productive in bone tools, bone heads, a few bone ornaments, one burial, 210 arrowheads, 61 flint knives, 18 chert knives and a few odds and ends, all being in a very fine state of preservation. Not a great deal of pottery came from this refuse heap, all of it being of the late Heart River type. Some very crude flint and chert was also found, one 3¾ pound celt came from the top of the burial; the burial was in a sitting position, probably a teenager. The burial pit was 36 inches in true circumference and extended to a depth of about 40 inches from the clay bottom of the refuse heap. The smaller refuse heap contained but a few flint knives and a great deal of pottery fragments.

In 1952 exploration of the mound or refuse heap bordering the small creek at the north end was started. This heap protruded about four feet above the normal level of the terrain and had never been cultivated over, probably on account of its ashy surface, and height. We started taking the dirt from the top, about seven inches at a time, back and forth across the mound, continually finding the dirt very soft and no need for heaving digging, it was very dry and sieved readily.

From the beginning the mound proved very productive and the deeper we went the better it became. Heavy buffalo bones were found in profusion, also a great many deer and other animal bones, buffalo and deer probably being the main meat diet. Squash and gourd seeds were found throughout the entire mound, a great many charred corn cobs were also found at all depths.

By the end of 1955 we found the mound was 81 feet wide and 129 feet long, the central part had been dug to a depth of 14 feet and ash layers found all the way down, sometimes to a depth of 14 feet and ash layers were found all the way down sometimes just a foot apart and sometimes a bit more. Only two what looked like fireplaces were located. The mound contained four large cache pits and one small one. One of the large cache pits proved non-productive, the other three large ones contained buffalo bones, artifacts, both of stone and bone, and a great mass of pottery. No burials were found in any of the four large cache pits, although seven human skulls and five bundles of human bones were found at different depths of the mound. The last cache pit was found in October 1956. This contained a large amount of pottery, some very large-sized pieces and at the present time (December 1956), an attempt is being made to restore a whole pot from the fragments, four are well on the way to restoration. One large wolf skull was also taken from this pit.

During the four years that the exploration has been in progress, over 70,000 items have been taken from this mound, over four hundred tons of dirt has been hand sieved, using 24 x 72 inch screens. To date 15 screens have been worn out. The sieves were set up on iron pegs and worked with a hinge effect on one end, the dirt was shoveled into the screen and then worked through by hand until the dust and silt was all worked through the screen leaving only the heavier debris

---

On opposite page:
1, Long, split rib bone awl, smoothed over half way from tip toward butt end; 2, awl made from long bone splinter, well polished with a sharp point; 3, also made from split rib except that it is short and stubby with a rounded butt; 4, awl made from the cannon bone of a large bird; 5, 7, 8 and 9, other examples of bone awls; 6, awl or punch made from the large pectoral fin bone of a catfish, showing piercing at butt end; 10, beads made from the spinal bone of fish; 10 and 12, scoria beads; 13 and 14, shell beads used for adornment; 15 and 16, bone beads made from bird bones; 17, bone effigy made from the solid bone of an animal; 18, bone fishhook, having small groove for tying, with no barb; 19, fishhook blank on tabular-shaped slab of bone from which fishhooks were made; 20, game stone made from pottery; 21 and 24, bone game piecees, made from deer antler with none of the

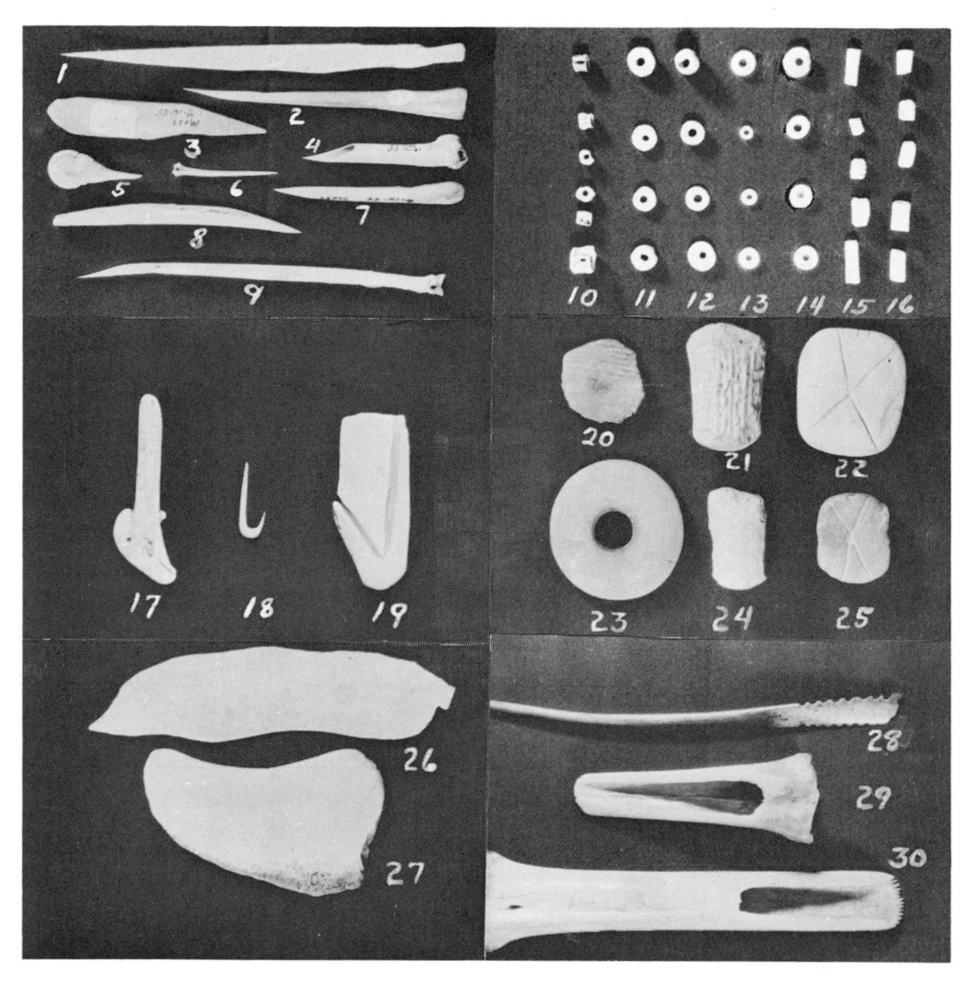

core removed; 22, scoria game piece, incised from corner to corner; 23, catlinite game piece, sometimes called a doughnut; 25, stone game piece made from prairie boulder, cross-corner incision on one side; 26, a short ovoid bone knife or scraper made from a bison scapula; 27, as above, but with supporting process left on; 28, long bone hair pin; 29, flesher or gouge made from bison radius bone; 30, flesher or gouge made from bison metacarpus, distal end cut away and end beveled to a cutting edge which is serrated. All artifacts from M. P. Mosbrucker collection, Mandan, North Dakota except 28 which was given to the author by the James Russell's of Dayton, Wyoming.

which was carefully looked over for whatever it might contain. Thus we think that nothing could have been overlooked, the screen was of such fine mesh that even small beads could not get through the mesh.

Items taken from the mound consisted of pottery, buffalo skulls, wolf skulls, human skulls, human bones, buffalo bones, deer bones, bird bones, a great many unidentified animal bones, arrowheads, spearheads, war points, flint and chert knives, bone knives, bone awls, bone needles, bone effigies, bone fleshers, bone digging sticks, bone flakers, bone beads, bone bracelets, bone head ornaments, bone gouges, bone fishhooks, scapula digging tools, bone shaft straighteners (these may have been bundle carriers), turkey and eagle bone whistles, and many other bone articles. Also found were flint and chert scrapers, shell beads, bone beads made from bird bones, scoria beads, stone beads, clay beads, flint game stones, catlinite game pieces, shell game pieces, buffalo shoulder-blade shovels and hoes, charred corn cobs, gourd seeds, squash seeds, wild fruit pits, nearly a ton of pottery fragments, celts, stone hammers, hammerstones, axes, flint drills, pumice abraders, bone abraders, copper points, copper dangle ornaments, copper beads, bone dangle ornaments, clay beads, pierced elk teeth, wolf teeth, deer teeth, buffalo teeth, buffalo jaws, wolf jaws, a variety of animal jaws, beautiful shell ornaments, stone effigy, and animal effigies worked into the design on the pottery. This is just a partial listing of what came from this mound during the years from 1952 to 1956 inclusive.

Why were all these beautiful artifacts thrown into this refuse heap? That is a question that has been bothering us for the entire time we have worked at the mound. Two or three reasons have been advanced by reliable authorities, but after studying the culture of the Mandan Indians, their habits, their religions, their beliefs, their superstitions, we

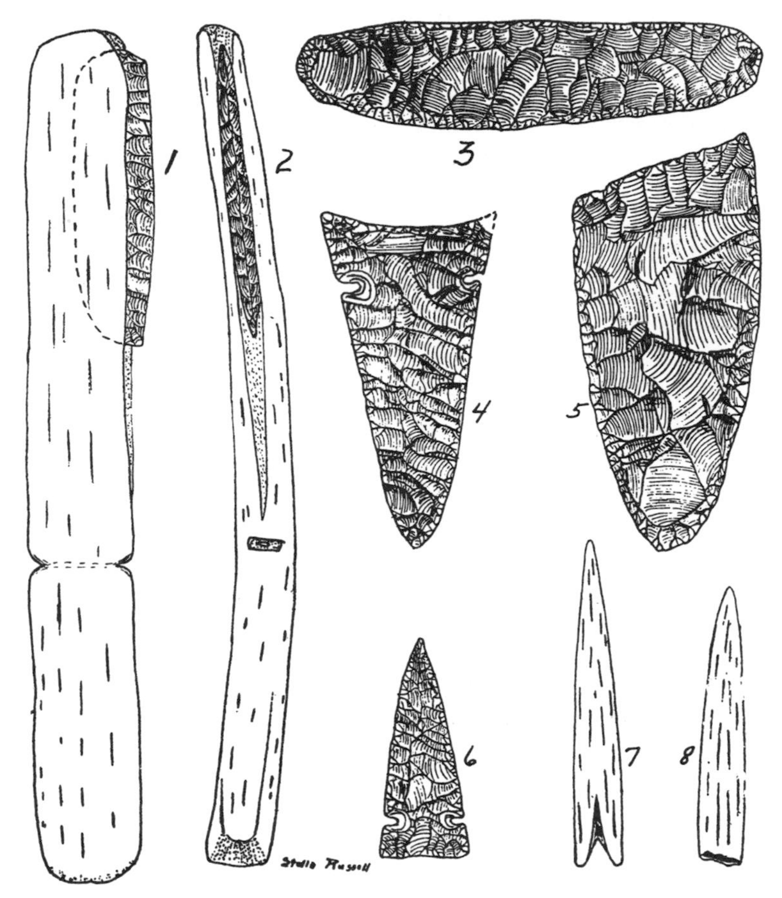

1 and 2, a knife handle made from a deer rib with one side incised so that a stone blade can be inserted, as shown, the hole permitted a method for carrying; 3 and 5, are examples of the beautiful workmanship of the Mandan Indians on stone knives; 4 and 6, two Mandan Indian arrowheads, showing the fine flaking which was characteristic of their stone work; 7, four-sided, bone dart point used in the game of darts, feathers being inserted in the hollowed-out end and the dart was hand-thrown; 8, round, bone dart point used when the Indians were competing with each other to see how many arrows could be shot into the air before the first one shot returned to the ground, or how many he could have in the air at the same time. All artifacts sketched from actual specimens from M. P. Mosbrucker Collection, Mandan, North Dakota.

still have not come up with a reasonable excuse as to why all these artifacts were discarded.

See photos and sketches of a few of Mr. Mosbrucker's Mandan artifacts on pages 41, 43 and 135.

CHAPTER 4

HOW TO DISPLAY THE COLLECTION

THE method used in preserving and caring for the artifacts you have found and bought is one of the most important things in building your collection. If care and pride is not taken to preserve and display the collection obtained, all interest will soon be lost. If the owner does not show pride and interest in his collection no one else will. This chapter will not attempt to mention all of the methods used by outstanding collectors, but will discuss a few suggestions for displaying your artifacts.

First, it is necessary to consider the amount of room for the display. If there is sufficient room, nothing is better than an electrically lighted show case. Cover the shelves with black or red velvet, which always gives that rich, luxurious effect, adding much to the pieces displayed. The size of the case naturally depends upon the size of the room. Do not hesitate to spend a little money for display purposes, for much money has been expended in time, gasoline, tires, etc., in obtaining the artifacts.

There is also the picture frame method. The back of the frame is lined with cotton, linen, velvet, flannel, or plain, highly polished boards, and the artifacts are fastened to the back either by wire, glue, rawhide thongs, or other desired method. The individual artifact may be mounted in a separate frame. The size naturally depends upon the size of the artifact to be displayed. It is well to have a colorful Indian blanket or rug to hang on the wall as a background. Drapery hooks can be put into the blanket and the individual frames hung in pleasing arrangements.

There are those who use an open set of shelves, usually highly varnished. Friends may come in and handle and minutely inspect each piece when the artifacts are displayed in this manner. The disadvantage to this is that some careless person may drop a priceless piece and all he can say is, "I'm sorry!" But that will not restore the artifact.

You may use a set of small drawers. The type used by department stores to keep thread in, makes a good set. These drawers are compact and do not take up much room. Line the bottom of the drawer with cotton or material and fasten your artifacts in. They can be shown by removing the drawers one at a time.

There is the method of using a highly polished board and fastening the artifacts onto it. By boring holes in it, the artifacts can be fastened to this board or shield by wire or buckskin thongs. The board can be cut into various attractive shapes, such as an arrow head, star, circle, Indian head or other design.

One collector took a roll of ordinary cotton, unrolled it, placed in an artifact and began rolling the cotton up again, in a very tight roll. The artifacts could not touch each other and break by contact. If this method is used, considerable care must be taken to roll them in tightly and then tie cords around the roll when completed to be sure to hold them in place.

Then there are fountain pen boxes, jewel boxes, jewel trays, and similar cases which can be used to display very valuable and outstanding pieces. If the collector considers his artifacts as jewels, they will be treated as jewels by those who view them.

There are many small display cases like fountain pen, watch, pipe and cosmetic cases that may be purchased at drug

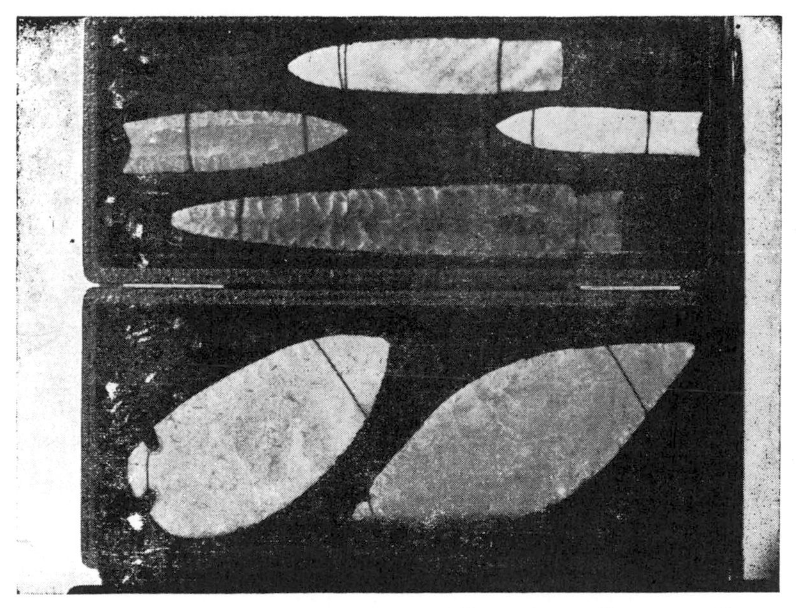

A quality collection containing a few choice pieces. Top row, Yuma; second row, Folsom and Yuma; third row, beautiful 6-inch Yuma specimen; bottom row, delicate, corner tang knife, and leaf-shaped knife. V. Y. Russell Collection, Casper, Wyoming.

A popular spot for the local Boy Scouts is that attractive den of "Buck" Burshears, La Junta, Colorado.

stores and confectionary stores. They frequently have more than they need and are willing to sell them reasonably.

The method frequently used is the old cigar box, shoe box or even the old tin can into which the pieces are unceremoniously "dumped." If the collector does not prize his pieces why doesn't he give or sell them to someone who will cherish and value them?

These are only a few of the many methods of mounting and preserving a collection but they will give a beginning collector some ideas. If he is at all ingenious, many other novel and interesting ways may be found to display his hobby.

CHAPTER 5

PRESERVING BROKEN ARTIFACTS

THERE are thousands of pieces of artifacts and broken artifacts found to every complete one which is added to a collection. Collectors always keep the complete piece but far too many of them scorn the broken artifact. This is a great loss to archaeology, for as far as the true scholar is concerned the pieces are practically as valuable as the whole artifact. It is the purpose of this chapter to encourage collectors to save their pieces.

First, consider the broken piece that is all there. It can be glued together and put into the collection of other whole artifacts. Then there is the piece that is only partly missing. Take some plastic wood, build it up to its original shape. It may take some time to do this but with practice you will become very proficient. Some collectors will object to this method and say "fraud" or "fake." No, it is not the purpose of this method to fool, misrepresent or deceive. It is done so that one may get an idea of what the original was like. It will make many pieces, of otherwise little value, greatly appreciated. It is known fact that many of the skeletons and remains in the museums are "built up"; that is, many of the bones are missing, and so these missing pieces are supplied artificially. This method is used in order that people may see what these prehistoric animals looked like. Many things we see in a museum are re-built in some manner. Even mounted animals and birds have eyes, tongues and parts which are artificial.

It is desirable to make a notation on the artifact, that it

is rebuilt. This will save thousands of beautiful pieces from being lost or thrown away. There is an opportunity for several people to work up a good business of rebuilding Indian artifacts for collectors. They could term it an "Artifact Hospital."

Many people think they find pieces which are in reality complete artifacts. A good example of this is the Yuma point. It does not have a hilt like the majority of other points; many amateur collectors, or sheep herders find it and think it has not been completed. They then attempt to work a hilt on it, thereby ruining a very valuable piece.

Broken artifacts? Yes, just broken artifacts but they, too have a distinct value, both educational and commercial. The "factory" that turns out genuine Indian artifacts is shut down. The number of authentic pieces are not increasing, but actually decreasing, caused by loss and deterioration. However, the demand is increasing by leaps and bounds. Each year thousands of new collectors, hundreds of these are youth organizations such as Boy Scouts, Girl Scouts and others, demand artifacts for study.

The cost of complete artifacts is prohibitive for these organizations to purchase. There are not enough inexpensive ones to go around. A few collectors have seen this problem and are trying to help solve it by gathering up pieces of artifacts and selling them to youth groups at a figure they can afford. One of the pioneers in this field was Frank V. Linker of Danville, Pennsylvania. He continually searched for collectors who cared little for "just pieces," and gathered these together so that when amateurs or groups wanted a representative collection of artifacts, they could secure specimens at a price they could afford to pay. He classified and identified the pieces so that they were just as valuable from the educational viewpoint as the complete artifacts. They retain the fascination of the complete artifacts, for the boys and girls

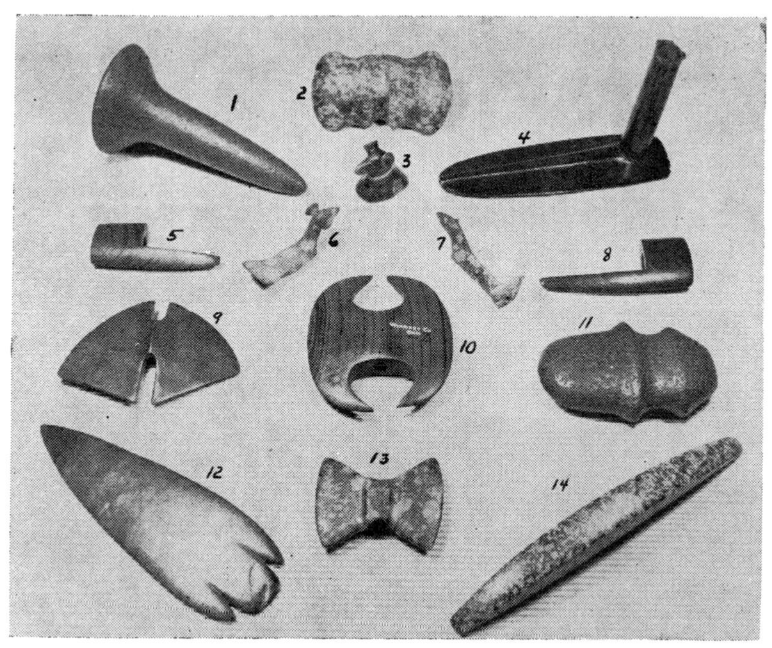

These fine specimens are from the extensive collection of the late F. G. Burdette, Springfield, Ohio. 1—Large pestle $9\frac{1}{2}$ inches tall, marvelous in size and design, Van Wert Co., Ohio; 2—double bitted quartz axe with jasper spots of pink, Indiana; 3—amazing bird stone with quartz collar and jasper pink spots; 4—very rare stone pipe, Mason Co., W. Virginia; 5 and 8—unusually large geniculates $5\frac{1}{4}$ to $6\frac{1}{8}$ inches long, Muskingum Co., Ohio; 6 and 7—fine porphery bird stones from Miami Co., Ohio; 9—rare butterfly banner $6\frac{3}{4}$ inches long, Darke Co., Ohio; 10—marvelous double crescent banner stone $6\frac{1}{2}$ inches in diameter, Wyandot Co., Ohio; 11—remarkable red jasper axe, Michigan; 12—very unusual grave find from Maine 11 inches long of slate; 13—rare porphery 'necktie' banner stone, Illinois; 14—remarkable speckled ceremonial pick $12\frac{1}{4}$ inches long, rare specimen from Ohio.

know that these pieces were made, owned and used by real Indians.

Since the price of artifacts has gone up, many "fakes" are being made and sold. It is certainly commendable that collectors and dealers are making an effort to find useful resting places for their broken pieces which greatly outnumber the perfect specimens.

Mr. M. W. Hill of Alexandria, Virginia has written the following on the repair of Indian artifacts:

"These brief comments sum up some of my experiences in making repairs to over a thousand artifacts.

"Repairing a broken piece when none of the parts are missing is not difficult but may take a lot of time if the parts are numerous, as a good slow setting glue is best for a permanent job. Remember always that most glues break down under conditions of dampness. I repaired some large porcelain jars and they stood up well for years until I put them down in the cellar, which is reasonably dry; there they collapsed. It is advisable to shellac over glued repairs to keep out dampness; in hollow objects shellac should be applied both inside and outside.

"When large portions of an artifact are missing they can most accurately be replaced by making a cast of the original part using plaster of Paris or cement, then trimming it to fit the original part; it may then be glued into place and colored to match.

"When smaller portions of the artifact are missing, replacements can be made by using many plastic materials. One of the best is putty and glue; it is messy to handle but it sets hard and takes coloring well. Its one fault is that it becomes brittle.

"Mending wood is easily worked and is suitable for repairing small nicks and dents, but must be applied in thin layers and built up to the necessary thickness. As this wood shrinks a good deal in drying and does not adhere well to stone materials, so it often comes loose and has to be cemented into place again. It takes coloring well and can be roughened or polished to suit.

"The most difficult repairs are to artifacts which are of solid color or clear and translucent. Repairs are hard to conceal on solid colored artifacts if a sizeable patch is to be made. The clear materials are the hardest of all to repair and the only thing I have found to match them is Plexiglas which takes dyes and is transparent. When the clearness is to be reduced to translucence a fine emery will produce the cloudiness desired.

"Water colors are better than oils for coloring but need a fixative to prevent rubbing off. I have experimented with half a dozen so called "crystal clear" liquid cements but none used so far remain white clear, all cure with a yellow cast, some even opaque wax color. The matching of flints of mixed composition is not so difficult as the solid colors because the streaking, spotting or dotting can be simulated with a fine brush and water colors. Again, this work of mottling must be protected by a shellac or other fixative or the coloring will be destroyed when the piece is cleaned or washed.

"For filling scars, dents or other damage to the large pieces as axes, celts, etc., one of the several iron cements as used by heating contractors will make a tight patch, brown or black in color, but can be colored to match the flint.

"One thing which must be remembered is the tendency to curl or pull out of alignment of light parts when any of the volatile liquid cements is used. The outside skin dries before the inner cement and a surface tension is set up that pulls light parts out of their position. Light weights or spring clips may be used to hold the parts where they belong until the final setting takes place."

CHAPTER 6

ARTIFACT PICTURES

THERE are thousands of collectors of Indian artifacts who get their specimens the hard way—finding them. These persistent "artifact hounds" spend their week ends, evenings and vacations tramping mile after mile over prairie, sand blow, old lake beds, in caves, over mountains and through canyons, searching for the elusive artifact. They find about one hundred pieces or flint chippings for each complete artifact. These pieces are carried home and placed in an old box, can or jar and soon forgotten.

It is a pity that these beautiful pieces are discarded. A few people have found a solution. They use these pieces for their own satisfaction and in some cases to their profit. They paint artifact pictures.

First, the collector arranges all of the pieces into piles according to their colors; reds, browns, greens, blacks, whites, creams, pinks, tans, grays, crystals, and others.

Second, the collector decides what picture he wants to "paint." Often it is an Indian head, a buffalo, an Indian pony or whatever subject might appeal. Then a large picture frame is secured.

There are various materials which may be used for the background, depending upon the picture—velvet canvas, flannel or straight cotton batting. Fasten this firmly on the back of the picture frame or on any board. Then sketch the picture you want to make. Start "painting" by putting glue on each piece or artifact or chip as it is put into its place in the "picture." Great care must be taken to select the pieces as to color, material and size. The picture may be just an outline or it may be completely filled in with chips and pieces, containing skillfully blended colors and detail. It is suggested the pieces may be waxed or a coating of shellac put on them to bring out the luster of the stone.

This method of utilizing pieces and flaking saves many valuable specimens, gives one a work of art, and places them together so that they may be displayed to the public in pleasing form. There is no satisfaction in showing a quart jar full of chippings, or pieces of arrowheads but an "artifact picture" can be shown with great pride of achievement.

A man in Lamar, Colorado, has twenty-five "artifact paintings." They are enclosed in large frames, and are beautiful pictures to behold. I have heard that he has been offered large sums of money for them.

Every collector who hunts his artifacts has thousands of such pieces. You can usually get him to give them to you or trade for several hundred of them by giving a few good artifacts. Get busy, collectors, save and use your pieces and chippings of flint. If you do not want them, give them to others who do.

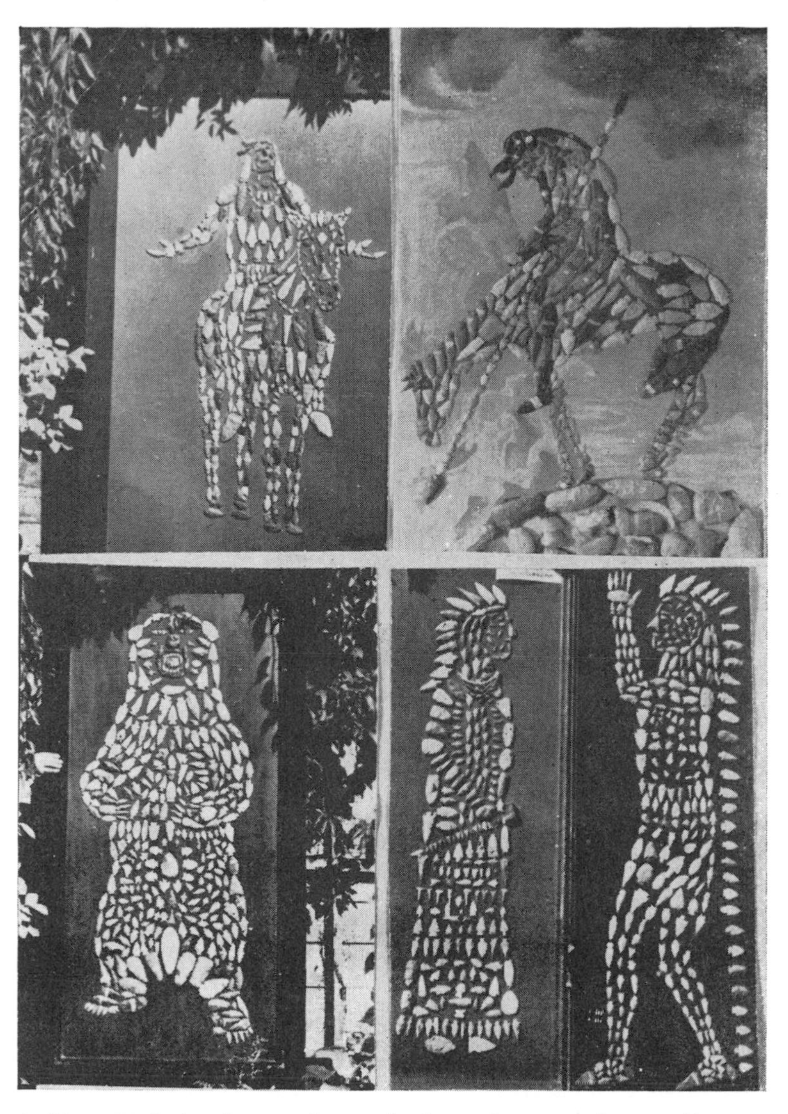

Artifact "Paintings" may be made by using complete artifacts or pieces, whichever suits the fancy of the "painter." Shown here are skillful reproductions of the famous paintings "Plea to the Great Spirit" and "End of the Trail." A background has been painted back of the picture "End of the Trail." These "paintings" were done by the late Dr. A. R. Wittman, of Merrill, Wisconsin, and are now owned by his son, C. R. Wittman, Crandon, Wisconsin.

CHAPTER 7

RESOLUTIONS FOR AN ARTIFACT COLLECTOR

1. I resolve to take better care of my collection. I will carefully wrap each unmounted piece.

2. I will study the various ways of mounting a collection. Then I will mount all of my collection so that it may be preserved for posterity.

3. I will go over my collection and cull out all specimens I do not really want. I will either sell, trade, or give these pieces to some one who does want them and will take good care of them.

4. I will do everything possible to encourage the people of my locality to start a museum where Indian artifacts may be displayed and kept safely through the years. If a museum is already in existence in my locality I will endeavor to start a club of collectors who will help build up the museum as well as their own collections.

5. I will decide how I am going to dispose finally of my collection. I realize I cannot go on forever but my artifacts will. I have seen many fine collections thrown away when the owner died. There was no one in the family who appreciated them. I resolve this will not happen to my collection. The specimens are only in my hands for a comparatively brief time—many other owners have had them. So I will keep faith and see to it that these valuable specimens are not broken, lost, or destroyed during my ownership.

6. I will carefully catalog my collection. I will number each specimen and write all I know about it—who first found

it, when, where and all the other details I can find on it. If necessary I will write many letters to obtain this information.

7. I will try and add to my collection. If I do not increase my collection I will start to lose interest.

8. I will try to get other collectors interested in going out into the field to search for artifacts.

9. If I make a find of a site, a depth find, I will notify my university or some local educational institution so they can come, study it, and carefully evaluate the material—artifacts, bones, charcoal and other material which may be found. If the first institution is not interested, I will notify others. It is well to notify my own state university or the Smithsonian Insitution in Washington, D.C.

10. I will study books, magazines, pamphlets, and learn all I can about the Indian and his work.

11. I will try to get laws passed making it a felony to make, imitate and pass off white man made artifacts as Indian artifacts.

12. I will *not* keep my specimens in old tin cans, cigar boxes, or fruit jars, where they will bump against one another and be chipped or broken. If I do not value them enough to care for them I will see that they get into the hands of someone who will appreciate and care for them.

13. I will strive for quality in my collection—not just quantity.

14. If I decide to give my collection to a museum I will see if they have a place to display my collection, not just room to store it away in a barrel or some old carton. If they agree to display my collection, will they give me a signed statement to that effect? If not, find some museum that will. Many museums have much of their material stored away. The artifacts may never be displayed—depending upon the "whims" of the curator. It is well to have my collection housed as soon as possible, while I am still living.

A small part of Verne Mokler's outstanding collection, Casper, Wyoming. Third frame, second row of small frames contains two very rare corner tang drills. In front of the frames are—a stone ring, tube pipe, war club, tomahawk, moccasin last, spear and pipe; also several bone and walrus ivory harpoon points from Alaska.

15. I will consider it just as praiseworthy to find a specimen in the hands of someone who does not want it, and it is letting it gather dust, as to find it in the field, providing he can furnish me with a complete history of it.

16. If I find a good hunting place, I will let other collectors know where it is—if not immediately I will do so as soon as I am through with it. I will record all this in my notes so that future collectors may benefit from it.

117. I will lecture, talk, write and do all possible to create an interest in the study of, and collecting of, everything Indian. I will display my collection at Stone Age Fairs or any time a local merchant wants me to do so, providing he furnishes a proper place for protection against handling and theft.

18. I will not throw away the broken pieces but will try to find someone who wants them. Broken pieces make very good Indian artifact pictures.

19. I will try to help others build up their collections and not discourage and hinder beginners from starting a collection as some "envious" collectors do.

20. I will do all I can to get collectors acquainted with one another. There are many lone collectors miles from others who will be cheered and encouraged by correspondence and visits from other collectors.

21. I will be careful to whom I lend my artifacts for study and examination. I am always ready to help those genuinely interested but must be careful not to let "just anyone" have them for study—I may never see the specimen again.

22. I will mount my collection with the thought of permanence and protection as well as beauty and display.

23. I will join at least one archaeological society to gain more knowledge for myself and to lend impetus to their work by increasing their numbers and lending support.

PART TWO

INDIAN ARTIFACTS IDENTIFIED

CHAPTER 8

OUTSTANDING INDIAN ARTIFACTS

THE BANNER STONE

IT seems that one of the most highly prized artifacts—or possibly *the* most highly prized artifact in collections east of the Mississippi River—is the banner stone. The individual collection is rated by the number of banner stones it contains.

There are numerous shapes and designs of banners. Some are rectangular, reel-shaped, crescent-shaped and of a butterfly design. Probably the butterfly design is the most highly prized. This type gets its name from its resemblance to a butterfly with expanded wings.

The banner stone seems generally to be thought of as a ceremonial stone, though I have heard some say it was a "peace stone," used as we use the flag of truce. It was placed on a stick, held up, and the warrior advanced as our soldier does under the flag of truce.

They are highly polished and show highly developed workmanship. One of the best collections of banner stones is owned by Dr. T. Hugh Young of Nashville, Tennessee.

Since these stones are so rare and sell for big prices, many attempts have been made by the "white brother" to duplicate them and cash in on his red brother's ability to turn out fine specimens of stone work. This recalls to mind the statement:

"An Indian scalps his enemy but a white man skins his friend."

Banner stones are pictured on pages 29, 51 and 67.

THE BIRD STONE

One of the most highly prized artifacts found in the north central part of our country is the bird stone. The collectors in that part of the country prize them as the western collector does his Yuma and Folsom artifacts. The majority of bird stones have been found in Michigan, Ohio, Indiana, New York, Wisconsin and Illinois. A few of them have been found in the eastern and southern states. Quite a few are reported to have been found in Canada. This artifact is a replica of a bird and is usually of very highly polished slate or argillite.

The big question concerning the bird stone is what was it used for? The most prevalent theory is that they were worn as an ornament, just as people today wear various ornaments with no significance. Some authorities believe they were worn by married women and especially when they were pregnant, which was to give the prospective mother protection.

Other authorities believe they were worn by young girls on the threshhold of womanhood. They wore the bird stone to inform their suitors that they were now old enough to be considered as a mate.

We also find it stated that they were worn by members of a certain clan—probably the bird clan. The significance would be the same as lodge pins, rings and fraternal emblems of today. Some support the theory that it was the medicine man who had the privilege of wearing a fine replica of a bird. Or, it may have been worn as a good luck charm when hunting, especially when hunting water fowl.

There is also the possibility that they were fastened to the prow of a canoe or boat, just as the ancient boats and galleys carried their emblems on their prows.

Other theories are presented, but the ones just men-

A portion of the collection of Maynard A. Fisher, of Owensville, Missouri. A good example of some of the outstanding private collections over the country. The stray pieces and small collections are gradually gravitating to these large, private collections, and in time these collections will all find their way into the large public museums where they will be preserved for future generations.

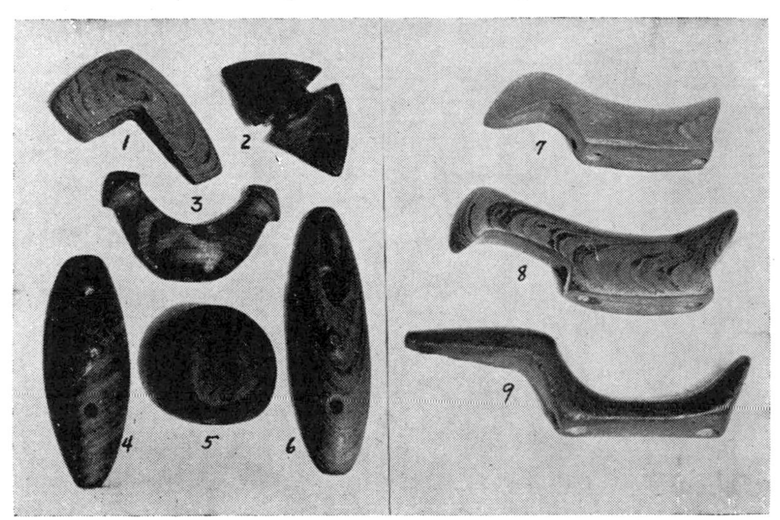

A few choice artifacts from the very fine collection of Mr. H. E. Fronville, Watseka, Illinois. 1—L Banner; 2—Butterfly Banner; 3—Phallic Banner; 4 and 6—Knobbed Gorgets; 5—Ball Banner; 7, 8 and 9—Fine Banded Slate Bird Stones. All are from Sandusky County, Ohio, except No. 3, which is from Indiana.

tioned appear the most believable. If more theories were presented here, it would probably tend to confuse collectors more than they are already on the purpose of the bird stone. It is doubtful if any other artifact has as many different theories as to its possible use.

It is rather unusual that the bird stone does not appear in western collections. The eastern arrows, knives, spears and various other specimens are purchased and traded to the West, but one rarely finds a bird stone. Two very fine bird stones were observed in a Denver collector's glass case, but on inquiry it was found that he had recently arrived from Columbus, Ohio. Dr. T. Hugh Young, of Nashville, Tennessee, has the finest bird stone collection I know of. It is truly outstanding. Illustrations appear on pages 51, 67 and 69.

THE DISCOIDAL

The discoidal is a circular, concave stone artifact found in various parts of the country but mainly in the north central part. They vary in diameter from one to nine inches and in weight from one ounce to twenty pounds, and are made from all kinds of quartz and variations of granite. The majority of them are concave on both sides; those which are concave on one side are comparatively rare. A few are flat-sided and are called the Biscuit type; others are perforated, and some have flanges around the edge.

Many believe that the Indians put them on the graves of their dead, placing food in the concave surface for the departed spirits. A modern Indian was asked if he believed that the spirits actually ate the food. He hesitated a moment then answered:

"You white people put flowers on the graves of your dead. Do you believe they smell the flowers? No? Well, we

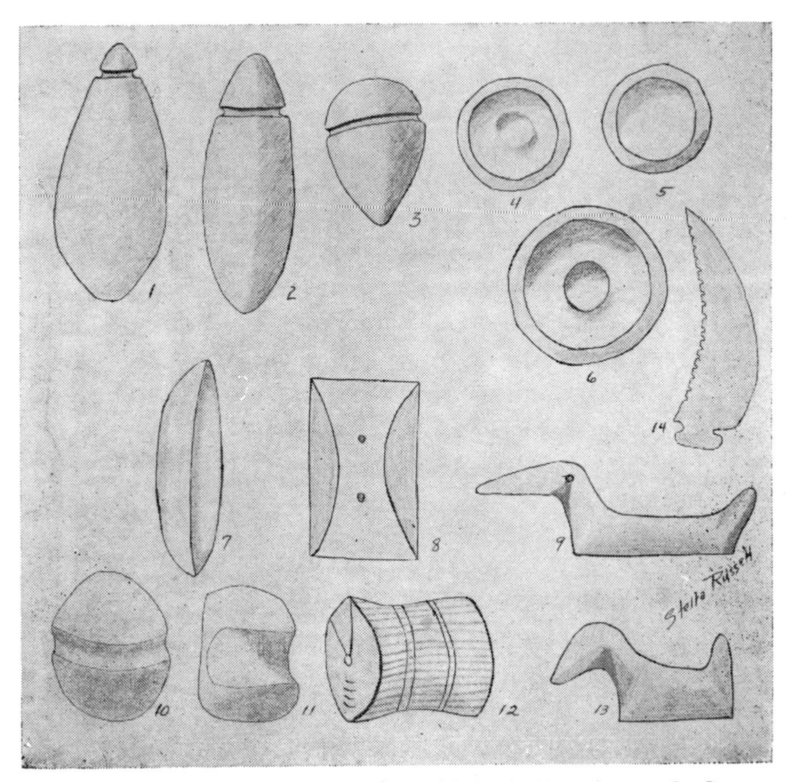

1, 2 and 3—Plummets; 4, 5 and 6—Discoidals; 7—Boat Stone; 8—Gorget; 9 and 13—Bird Stone; 10 and 11—Sinkers or Mauls; 12—Spool; 14—Stockton Curve.

put the food on the graves of our dead for the same reason."

One collector writes: "These marvelous discs are often made of fine quality material—even rose quartz—and are therefore beautiful objects for us to admire. They seldom ever show any checks or signs of having been used in a game or abused in any other way. The finest sentiments come from those who hold them in reverence as sacred discs on which sacrifices were offered to the high priest or medicine man for things they wished would happen."

Others say they were used as a small bowl in which herbs and seeds were mixed to make medicines.

Some claim they were used in games and known as "game stones." There was no one certain game; the games differed in various parts of the country and with different tribes. There are so many different stories of the games and how they were played that it is impossible to go into further detail in a book of this type. Ilustrations may be found on page 69.

THE BOAT STONE

The boat stone is found principally in the Great Lakes region, though, like every other artifact, it has wandered to other parts of the country. Thc boat stone is a replica of a boat or canoe, as the name indicates. It is not chipped, but is a highly polished artifact. The deeper the concave surface, the higher the polish and the better the material, the more highly prized the boat stone is.

An occasional boat stone is found west of the Mississippi River but the majority of them are in the Northeastern collections. One very fine boat stone collection is at Fowler, Colorado, owned by John L. Wyeth. It is worth going miles to see.

Some areas produce the boat stone undrilled, while in other places two holes are drilled through the "bottom" of

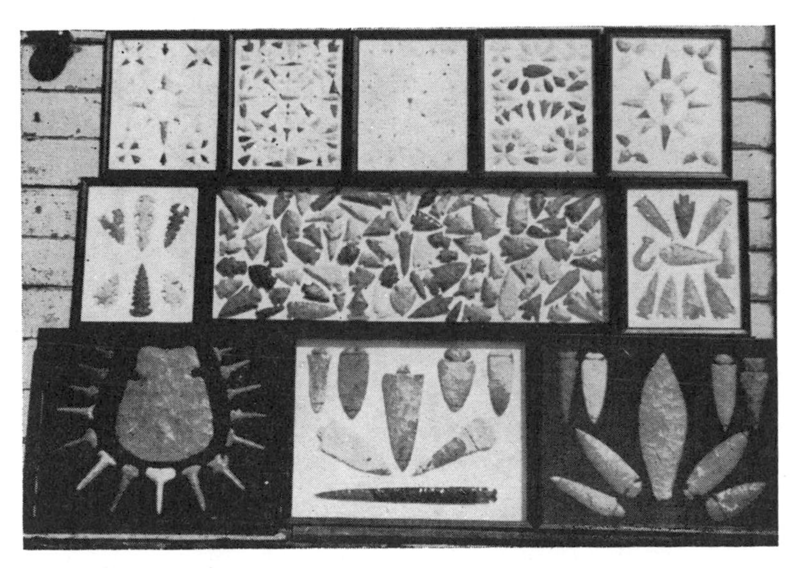

Attractively mounted display of fine artifacts ranging from tiny bird points (center frame, top) to large, well-made, notch hoe (lower, left frame). Other prominent artifacts–drills (around hoe), and serrated and effigy pieces (above hoe). A. W. Schlessing Collection, Huntingburg, Indiana.

Ladles made of pottery; stone rings or "doughnuts"; stone effigies. H. E. Fronville Collection, Watseka, Illinois.

the boat usually within three-fourths to one inch from each end.

There are various opinions as to the use of the boat stone. One is that the drilled boat stone was tied to the prow of the canoe or the boat, for an ornament, as the Indians prized ornaments and decorations of all kinds. Again, it may have been a "charm" to keep the boat from turning over in a storm or hitting a snag or rock which might mean catastrophe. It was also thought to bring good luck to the hunter or the fisherman. The undrilled boat stone was carried upon the Indian's person for the same purpose as the drilled one was placed upon the prow of the canoe. Boat stones were also found in Indian graves, probably to aid the departed spirit on its trip to the Happy Hunting Ground. Illustration is on page 69.

THE PLUMMET

The stone artifact called the plummet gets its name from its shape. The shape is very similar to a carpenter's plumbob, but the use of the artifact is far from that of the white man's plumbob which it so clearly resembles. Most of them are of hemitite although stone pieces are occasionally seen in collections.

Many tribes that did a lot of fishing undoubtedly used them as sinkers. They would certainly be very practical for this purpose. Many of them are found along the Pacific coast. In an old lake bed in Sonoma County, California, one man gathered five hundred in a few years.

Some authorities seem to believe the plummet was the stone of the medicine man. They were used to cure the sick and to bring rain. Some call them "rain stones." The medicine man held them tightly in the palm of his hand and when moisture appeared in the palm of his hand, caused by the

Top row—1, Blackfoot, two-piece pipe, no stem. 2 and 3, Sioux pipes of red catlinite. Second row—Two red catlinite pipes of recent origin. Third row—Iron and steel tomahawk with pipe bowl in head, hole through handle. Bottom—Fine pestle collection. The three white ones are of onyx. Double-bell pestle is green granite from Washington. Single knob pestle is of lava rock from Oregon. Long roller pestle is 18 inches long. Collection of the late C. A. Kinsey, Belgrade, Montana.

contact of the cool stone with his warm hand, he called attention to the moisture that gathered.

Some were worn as pendants, supposed to protect the wearer from numerous evils that were greatly feared.

Some authorities question their being used as sinkers or pendants because the ends are tapering and the grooves too shallow to hold a cord or thong no matter how tightly tied. These collectors believe they may have been encased in a skin bag and carried as pendants. Still others say they may have been used as bolas. Lashed together, one on each end of a long thong, they could have been used to entangle the legs of wolves, deer or other animals they wished to capture. Illustrated on page 69.

SPOOLS

One unusual artifact is the spool. It gets this name from its resemblance to our modern spool. The majority of these spools are found along the Ohio River Valley. They are not plentiful.

One collector presents a seemingly logical theory of the use of these spool-shaped artifacts. He states that they are usually made of sandstone and usually had two designs—one on one end of the spool and a different one on the other. By using a sling shot prong and a pad soaked with walnut stain or a pad soaked with pokeberry juice, the Indian was quickly able to tattoo himself and be ready for battle or ready for the war dance with a minimum of delay. The ends of the spool had different designs and these were used to stamp the forehead and cheeks.

Another collector informs me that they sometimes are called ear spools. In burials, they are found beside the head. Also copper, copper-covered wood and baked clay ear spools

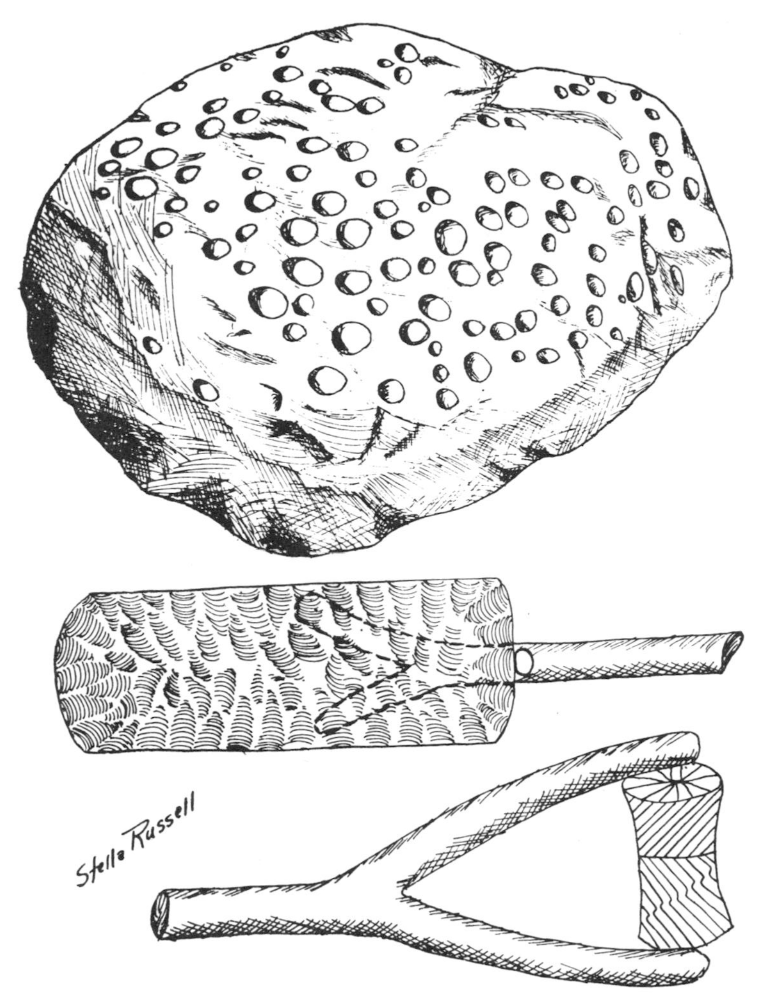

Top–Cup stone; Middle–Method of hafting spade (thongs were wrapped around the spade and stick, lacing it securely); Bottom–Spool with willow fork attached.

or ornaments are found with the Hopewell and Mississippi cultures.

Some call them a talisman or good luck piece. There is also the usual medicine man theory. It seems that when no other use can be found for an artifact, it is dismissed as being a tool of the medicine man. We also find some who believe they were used in playing certain games. Illustrations may be found on pages 69 and 75.

THE STOCKTON CURVE

A very rare artifact is found throughout California which has become known as the Stockton Curve as the first specimens were found near Stockton and were believed to have been an artifact of that area only. However, later they were found in many parts of California. It is a small curved specimen, usually made of black obsidian. The edges are usually serrated, sometimes only the curved edge is serrated. These specimens have very delicate workmanship which is similar to the workmanship on the so-called "gem" points. The majority of the Stockton curve pieces have been found in California. Quite a number of them have been found in Indian graves.

Collectors differ in their theories as to the use of the Stockton Curve. Many say they are ceremonials. This may be true, but it is too easy to call anything that is difficult to evaluate a ceremonial. One suggestion is that they were made to resemble the claws of an animal or the talons of a bird. They could be fastened on the fingers of the hand and give the wearer the ability to fight as a wild animal does. Other collectors believe they may have been used to scarify the flesh on ceremonial occasions. Illustrations may be seen on page 69

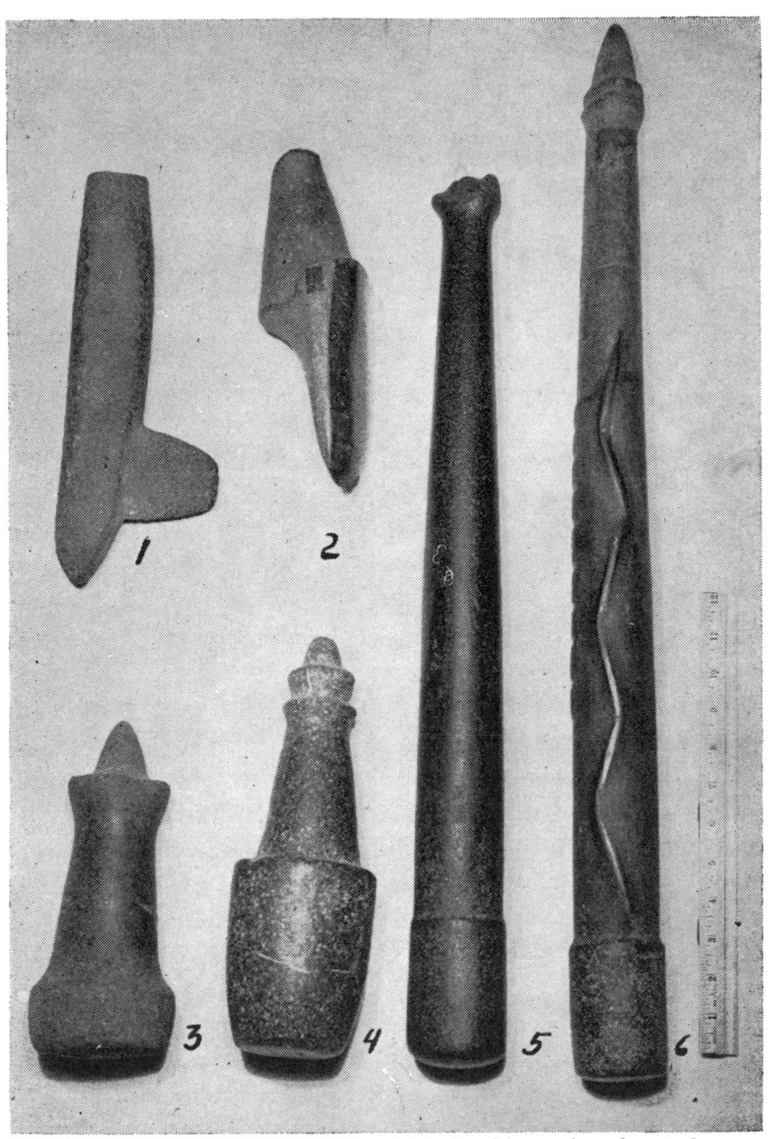

A few choice specimens of the Mid-Columbia region from the outstanding collection of Ernest Cowles of Grandview, Washington. 1—Axe with handle and blade made from one piece of stone. Grooved axes are seldom found along the Columbia River but several types of these Monolithic axes are found. 2—Celt with an offset handle, shaped somewhat like a brick trowel; the bottom is highly polished from long use. 3 and 4—Two pestles or hand mauls; early explorers state the Indians used these mauls to drive elk horn wedges to split firewood. 5—A 24-inch pestle with a bear head carved on top. 6—Pestle made of black basalt, 29 inches long with a snake carved in bas-relief on the side. Both 5 and 6 are very symmetrical and highly polished.

GORGETS

Gorgets are comparatively thin, flat specimens, but vary greatly as to their outline. They are frequently concave on one side and convex on the other, having holes drilled through them.

Authorities differ as to the use of gorgets. One theory is that they were worn on the left forearm to protect it against the slap of the bow string. They would also serve as a support, just as we wear leather supports on our arms and wrists. This theory is supported by the fact that gorgets have been found in graves, fastened to the left arm.

Some claim that it would be impossible to make a gorget that would be a good fit to the contour of the arm and would have to be bound so tightly to the arm to hold it in place that it would interfere with circulation and movement of the arm. Some claim it could have been used as a shuttle in weaving; some say it was a twine twister. Some believe it could have been worn suspended around the neck and hanging over the chest as a protector or ornament. There are so many different shapes and outlines that it is quite possible they had various uses. An illustration appears on page 69.

HOPEWELL ARTIFACTS

The origin of the Hopewell people, one of the most advanced prehistoric societies north of Mexico, is not known, but as long ago as 2,000 years they had developed their highly specialized civilization in the area of southern Ohio.

They were outstanding craftsmen and made copper breastplates, headdresses, earspools, beautifully carved stone pipes made to represent bird and animal life. Elaborate pieces buried with the dead were embellished with fresh water

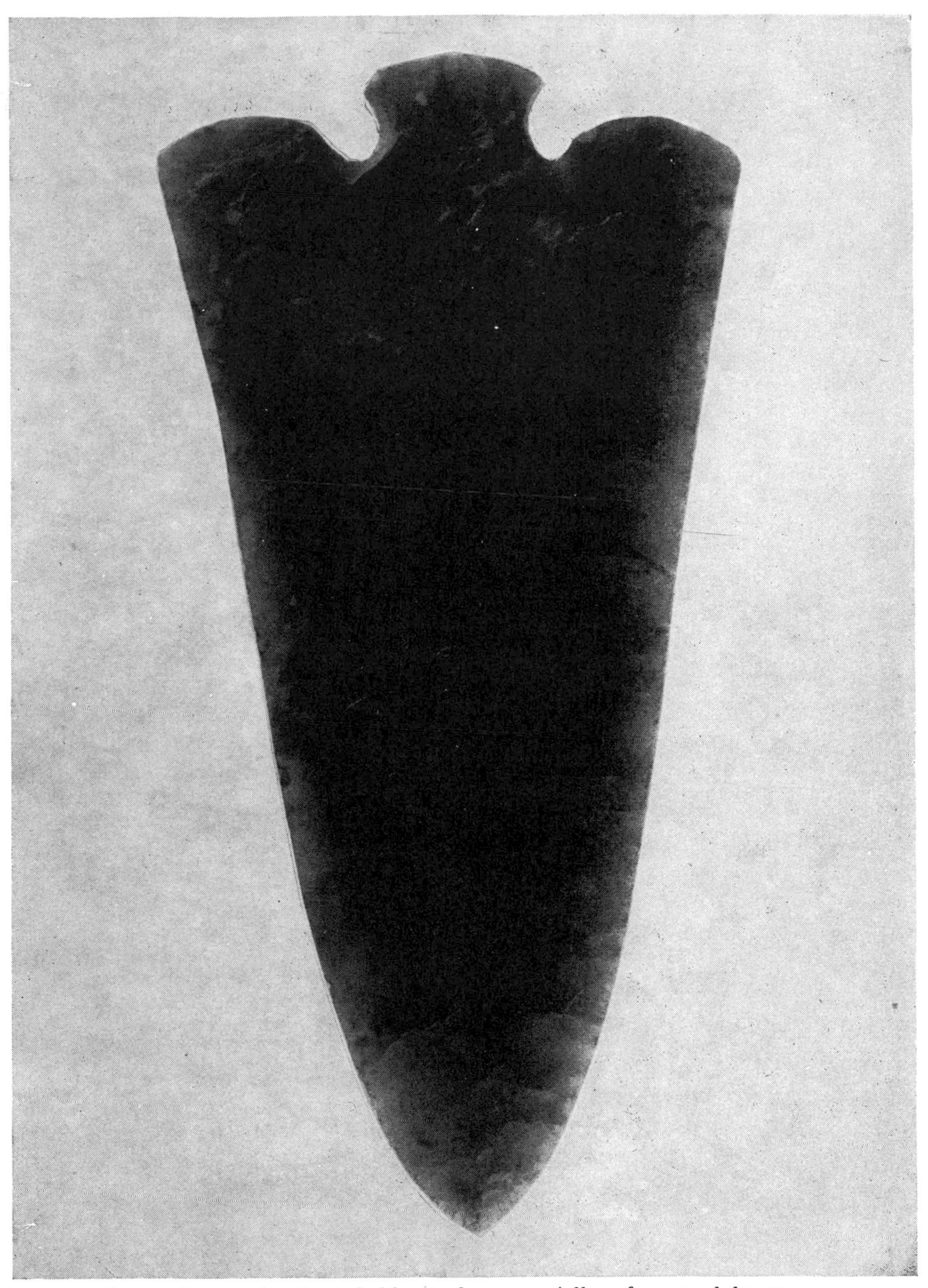

Hopewell spear-head, probably used ceremonially, of unusual beauty, from Calhoun County, Illinois. Material translucent amber color hornblend. Length, 6⅜ inches; width, 3⅛ inches. From Gray La Dassor collection. This cut courtesy Central States Archaeological Journal, Volume 2, Number 2.

pearls, quarts, mica, ocean shells and grizzly bear teeth. Excellent pottery was also made by the Hopewellians.

From obsidian, a volcanic glass brought from the Rocky Mountain region, they made delicately chipped ceremonial blades. See illustration on page 79.

CHAPTER 9

ARTIFACTS OLDER THAN THE INDIANS

THE YUMA BLADE

THE purpose of this chapter is to describe the Yuma blade so that the average collector will recognize a Yuma when he finds it. It is not intended to add anything new to the facts already known by scientists on the Yuma, but rather to assemble some of the facts and express them in terms that the collector who enjoys a few pieces will understand.

Let us begin with the statement that the Yuma, though one of the oldest artifacts in point of time, being from 10,000 to 15,000 years old, has not been known very long. Dr. A. E. Jenks was the first to direct attention to this point in about 1928 to 1930. He made a study of a collection of artifacts found by Perry and Harold Anderson of Yuma, Colorado. Shortly after this Dr. E. B. Renaud took up an intensive study of the subject and named the artifact "Yuma" in honor of the Colorado county in which the Anderson's artifacts were found. The Andersons dug most of their material, though some pieces were surface finds.

The Yuma is really not a point but a blade. Undoubtedly, it existed long before the bow and arrow and was used as a hafted blade, the haft being pieces of bone or horn. Examining the Yuma, you will find that the edge near the hilt is smooth or polished. The theory is that this was done to prevent the edge cutting the thongs or sinews that bound it to the handle.

Yumas are very scarce, probably more so than Folsoms. They are found in various parts of the country as surface finds, but the majority which have been unearthed have been found in Wyoming and Colorado with a few in surrounding states. They are usually found at a depth of from five to twenty feet. There are some surface finds due to erosion or movements of the earth's surface.

Yumas are of three distinct types: the oblique, collateral and indeterminate. The easiest to recognize is the oblique. It is a long, slim, triangular piece. The hilt or base is usually straight, convex or slightly concave. It is usually stemless. The chipping or flaking runs obliquely across the face of the blade. The ribbon-like chipping is parallel. The blade is thin and the more delicate the flaking, the better the blade.

Then there is the collateral Yuma which differs from the oblique in that the flaking usually runs to the mid-section and rises to a dorsal ridge. This ridge is frequently very pronounced. A cross section of the blade is diamond-shaped. A very fine specimen may be so well balanced that it will always come to rest on the dorsal ridge when placed on a hard, flat surface. The collateral Yuma is more frequently stemmed than the oblique, but the shoulders are indistinct. It is also a long, slim, narrow point.

The third classification is the indeterminate. This Yuma differs in that the edges are not parallel, but flare out a little past mid-section, finally coming to a more blunt or rounded point than the other types. The pattern of flaking is irregular and the workmanship is usually inferior to that found on the other two types.

Practically all Yumas have very fine tertiary chipping along the edge of the blade. It is very fine and delicate and is a method of sharpening the blade.

A point is often found which may reflect any of the three types classified above, but which has a hilt or base similar to what the modern Indian used. Many collectors cannot

Classic examples of the three types of Yumas. 1, Oblique Yuma, with a small break at the base, probably the most pictured of all Yuma blades, many replicas being on display at numerous museums throughout the country; 2, Collateral Yuma, showing beautiful parallel flaking; 3, Indeterminate Yuma, having distinct polish along edges of base and fine workmanship. 1, found by Perry Anderson, near Yuma, Colorado, it was among the first group studied by Dr. E. B. Renaud of Denver University who named them Yumas; 2, found in a sluice box in Montana in 1895; 3, found about 30 miles north of Lusk by Hans Gautschi of Lusk, Wyoming. All in the Russell Yuma Collection.

understand this. My theory is that the Yuma in question was found by an Indian and since he didn't keep a collection of points, he put it to more practical use. It was necessary to make a hilt with which he could fit it on the shaft, and he quickly chipped the notches and used it along with his other points.

Since my first two books were written, a lot of study and work has been done on the Yuma and various new sites have been worked. Some of these sites are the Scottsbluff, Eden Valley, Agate Basin and the Cody site. All of these have contained the collateral type of Yuma: that is, a dorsal ridge and parallel sides with the exception of the Agate Basin site.

There has been a tendency to designate Yumas by the name of the site in which they arc found. This would be a good idea if this type of Yuma was found only in this one location. However, these terms have come into such wide usage that I will give a brief description of each specimen.

The Scottsbluff Yuma is a collateral type of Yuma which is short, wide and might be termed the "fattest" of them all. *The Eden Valley Yuma* is a collateral type of Yuma which is long and slim, having been found in the Eden Valley of Wyoming. *The Cody* type is a colateral Yuma characterized by very heavy, bold flaking. It is more the shape of the Eden Valley but its flakes are much deeper and more bold in appearance. *The Agate Basin* type is an interminate Yuma, having irregular flaking. The site was found in the Agate Basin of northeastern Wyoming by Bob Frissen.

I have never heard that they ever located an oblique Yuma site, but one may be found at any time, possibly before this book goes to print. There were quite a few oblique Yumas found by Perry Anderson in his sites near Yuma, Colorado. However, this could hardly be called an oblique Yuma site as all three types of Yumas were found there. It

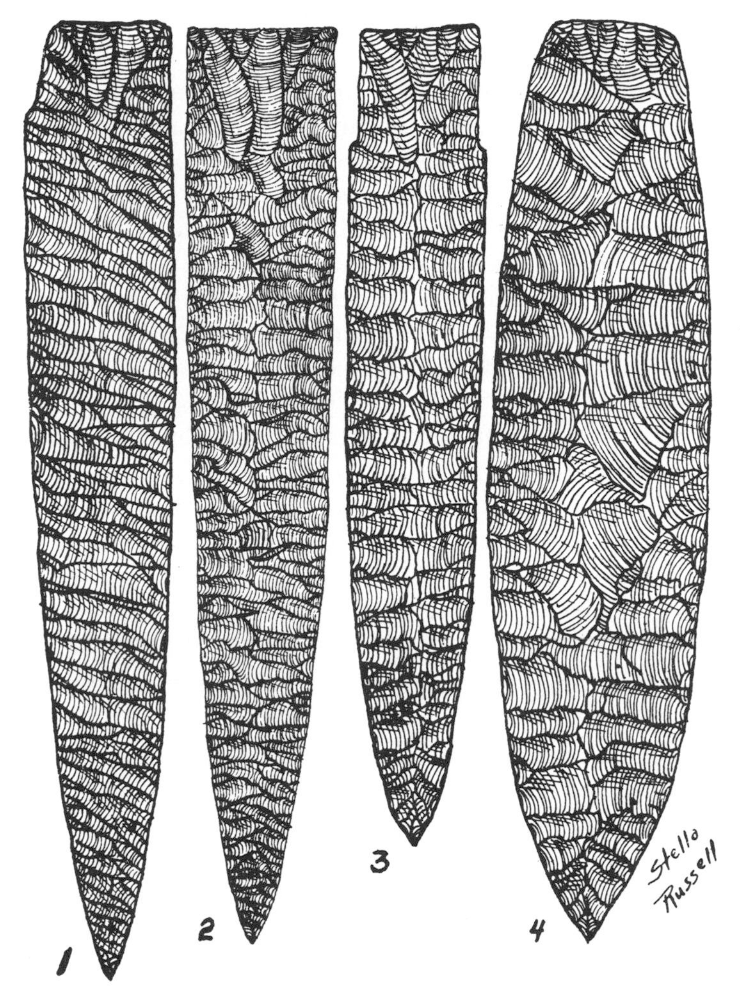

1—Oblique Yuma found by Perry Anderson near Yuma, Colorado;
2—Collateral Yuma found by Irwin Cox near Brush, Colorado;
3—Collateral Yuma found by Frank Scott near Douglas, Wyoming;
4—Indeterminate Yuma found by Hans Gautschi near Lusk, Wyoming.
—V. Y. Russell Collection.

seems that Mr. Anderson did not care to take any of the archaeologists of any university into his confidence and work with them. Therefore, very little is known of what I term the Anderson site, though it seems to me that the finest Yumas ever found came out of this site in Yuma County, Colorado.

Much value can be gained by the illustrations on page 62. If collectors will study this chapter and the accompanying illustrations, then study their own collections, they can determine to a reasonable degree of certainty whether or not they have any Yumas.

There are several ways of grading and determining the quality of a Yuma. Some determine it by the number of flakings per inch. I like to use the numerals 1 to 4 with the following values: 1—Superior, 2—Good, 3—Average, 4—Poor. Then take into consideration the following factors: A—Workmanship, B—Size, C—Material, D—Condition of Specimen, E—Color.

A. Workmanship: Prefer delicate, ribbon-like, uniform chipping. Check the tertiary chipping on the edge, the polish or smoothness of the hilt.
B. Size: They seem to vary in size from one to seven inches. A five inch blade is rare.
C. Material: Heavy, course material gives a crude piece. The finer the material, the better the specimen.
D. Condition: Many of the Yuma specimens are broken. A complete specimen is rare. Therefore the more perfect the condition the better the blade.
E. Color: Probably should not be considered, but the white, dull, creams and grays do not tend to make very beautiful artifacts.

The question most frequently asked about the Yuma blade is, "What is the value of a Yuma?" It is a question which is very difficult to answer. The answer depends on what it meant when you ask about the value. Do you mean scientific value or commercial value?

First, consider the scientific value of the Yuma. The Yuma has shown us that man existed on the continent many years ago; in fact, much longer than archaeologists thought for many years. The study of Yuma man's artifacts gives us some knowledge of the people—their habits, skills, tools and the life they probably led. New facts come to light as we unearth more Yuma tools.

The Yuma blade, to have the most value, must be one which has been unearthed at some depth. The history of the point must be known. Where was it found? Was it found with bones? What kind of bones? Who found it? Was he scientific enough to interpret its relationship to other things around it? When was it found? If possible, a picture should be taken of the blade before it is removed from the earth. A history answering all of these questions will add greatly to its scientific value. True, some of these facts are not always necessary, but the more of them that can be answered fully, the more scientific value the blade will have. Keep this information with the artifact and when it is transferred to another collection, supply the new owner with the data.

The surface find is not as valuable from a scientific viewpoint as the artifact which has been unearthed. If it is a surface find, it is impossible to determine the origin. Perhaps it was found, used, lost, found again and exchanged many times. Each owner probably carried it to a new location many miles from where it was originally found. In ancient times this transportation was carried on by Indian tribes. A surface find is of value in that it shows workmanship, the kind of material used, etc. Pieces of Yumas have about as much scientific value as the complete blade.

When the value means commercial worth in dollars and cents, the answer is entirely different. A good way to answer that is to ask what a watch, ring or precious stone is worth. It depends entirely upon the individual specimen. Watches and rings sell from a dollar up to thousands of dollars and so do precious stones. It all depends upon the specimen of which you speak. The same is true of a Yuma blade—from a dollar up to hundreds.

There are Yumas that can be bought for a dollar or two. These are "hard time" Yumas made of poor material and broken pieces, some with large chips out of them. These will help build up the bulk of a collection. One collector was known to ask $500 for a Yuma. He did not sell it. The highest price I know of that was ever paid was $250. This piece is out of the original Yuma collection of Mr. Perry Anderson. It is one of the finest ever found, has been shown in many museums, has won many prizes. It is a work of art. I have refused $300 for my best Yuma. However, as to the value of the average Yuma, it seems that it is from five dollars for ordinary blades to twenty-five dollars for very good ones. There is no real set value. The only way to make a deal is for the owner to say what the blade is worth to him; then, if the buyer values it more, a deal is made.

A statement is often made: "Well, if it is worth that to him, it is worth that to me!" Only a naive person would make such a statement. An artifact might be worth fifty dollars to a collector to fill out his collection and not be worth a cent to the owner who has no real appreciation of its history, workmanship, or archaeological worth. Of what value is a diamond to a savage? Yet to a dealer it is worth much. Of what value is a good pair of size six shoes to a man with a size eight foot? The moral is this: If you have some artifact, antique or other rare specimen that you do not prize or appreciate, let several collectors and dealers bid on it. Sell it to the highest bidder. Investigate, inquire from authorities, get a reasonable price and let it go where it will be appreciated,

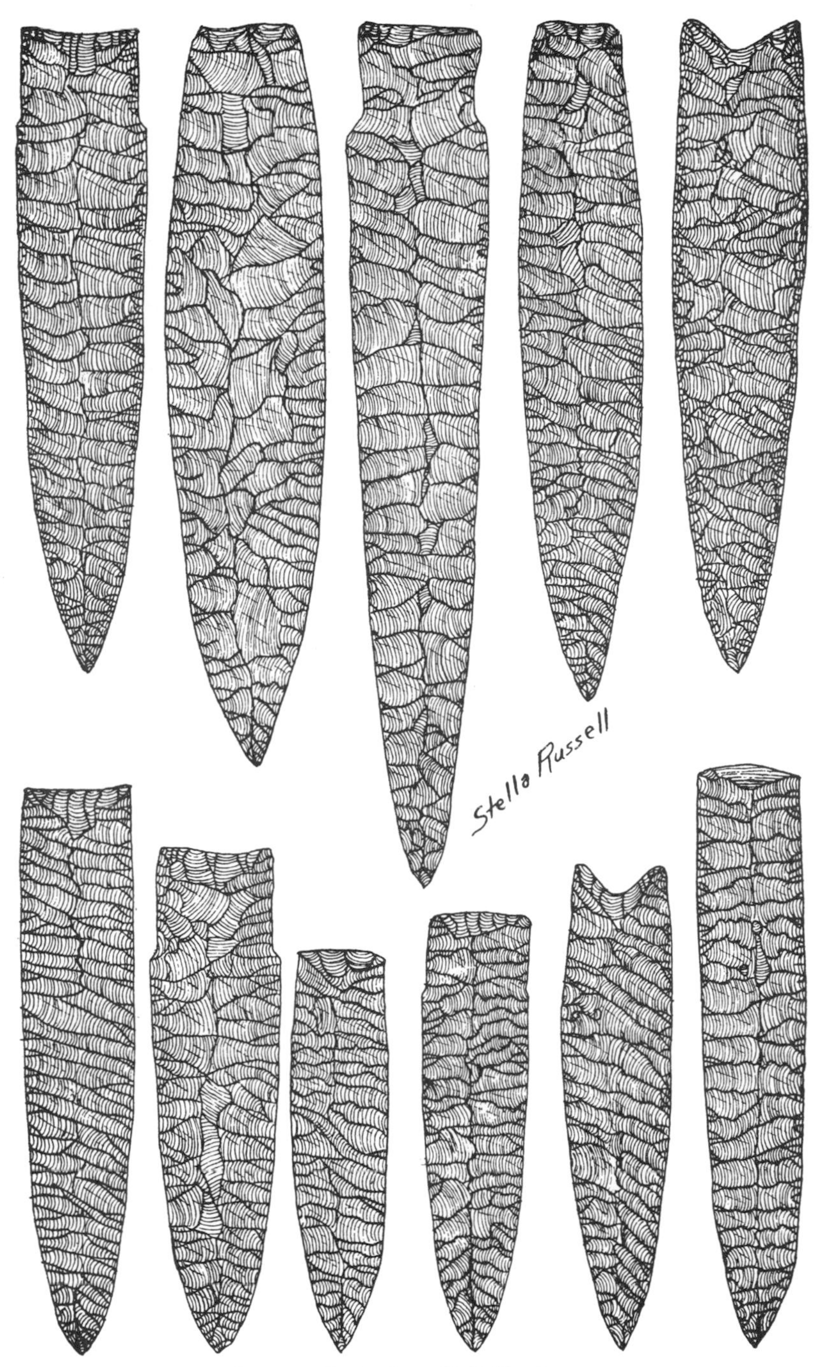

Yumas. V. Y. Russell Collection.

and will add to someone's collection. Don't be a dog in the manger, merely priding yourself in a possession for possession's sake. Some one else may really appreciate the specimen. This thought goes for relics and antiques of all kinds.

One of the purposes of the various magazines for hobbyists is to bring you names of dealers and collectors of all kinds of things, making it easy for you to get an answer to your question: What is my relic worth?

WHAT WAS YUMA MAN LIKE?

We write and talk about the Yuma, referring to the stone artifacts which we find, but what about Yuma man? Was he white, black, yellow or red? Where did he come from? Did he come from Asia as the majority of people believe the Indian did? Or did he originate here in the Western hemisphere? What became of him? Did a plague wipe him out? Why is it that we find no remains, such as his bones? Investigators of the future will answer these questions, I dare say, but so far scholars have only scratched the surface of this study.

I will not attempt to answer scientifically the question I have asked! I will only delve into the realm of possibility as I see it. Perhaps the reason no skeletons have been found of Yuma man is that he practiced cremation of the dead, thus erasing tangible trace of his people.

Artifacts reflecting the Yuma workmanship have been found from Alaska to Arizona. Masterpieces have been found in Wyoming and Colorado, east of the Rockies. It is possible that Yuma man came across from Asia and that as he progressed southward his skills increased.

The Aztecs and Mayans were a highly developed people and their stone work displays great artistic skill. Is it possible that the remnants of Yuma man migrated into Central America and founded another civilization?

Some of the various artifacts showing the Yuma workmanship are knives, spears, blades, chisels, awls, drills and other tools, whose use may be debatable. Many of these tools were undoubtedly used in many different ways, but all of them show the same beautiful workmanship and fine lines.

The general lines of any Yuma display pleasing symmetrical flaking, whether it be very wide or very narrow flaking. They show that Yuma man had a keen sense of balance, and possessed mental stability as a racial characteristic to be able to produce artifacts of such high quality. He had patience and skill of a high degree to turn out his tools so carefully. The entire surface of his tool was chipped with the same careful skill. Though the exact width of the flakes may vary, there is a flaking continuity characteristic to each point.

Each Yuma blade is well balanced. The majority may be placed on any hard surface, and when the edges are lightly tipped, the blade comes to rest on the center ridge. This shows that Yuma man must have been a person with keen intellect to discern the proportion of things—with mental stability and balance. He took great pride in his craftsmanship and had a love of perfection. A large, rough, coarse man could not have turned out this type of artifact. He would have turned out a heavier, cruder tool. Undoubtedly the maker of the fine Yuma point was an artist who possessed skill not attributed to the average Yuma man. His work gives evidence of the artistic taste of a civilized or semi-civilized being, for the work of savages is usually very crude. He showed a power of concentration and a quality of perseverance not demonstrated by the native American whom the white man found here.

Our imaginary Yuma man was perhaps of the same height as the average man of today, having the lean supple body and muscular development of the seasoned athlete, with full shoulders and long fingers on a strong hand. We can visualize his face as well-hewn and his forehead as high and well-developed like that of a thinker. We can imagine his skin bronzed and coarsened by wind, weather and sun. Clear eyes perhaps reflected the keenness of senses within, and discerned the beauty of things about him. Our image further shows the broad nose and prominent jaw of a man who constantly battles nature and the elements for survival, for great strength was needed to survive in a period of our world's existence when pre-historic animals roamed our plains.

Yuma man must have treasured the works of art that he made. And he must have been reluctant to throw them away, for he re-chippd them into other useful tools when they became broken. Yuma blades often give evidence of having been re-sharpened. This probably was done when a point was broken off. We find a hilt that should correspond with a five inch artifact, worked down to a drill, an awl or another useful tool, sometimes only one and one half inches long.

To me, Yuma man lived and breathed in the being described above; his real history remains to be solved by the scholars of the future.

PLAINVIEW POINTS

The Plainview points were originally found near Plainview, Texas, thus the name. These, in my humble opinion, may be of the Yuma complex. They have some of the characteristics of the Yuma without the fine flaking which is generally associated with Yumas. See illustration on page 97.

FOLSOMS

One of the most sought after artifacts is the Folsom. It

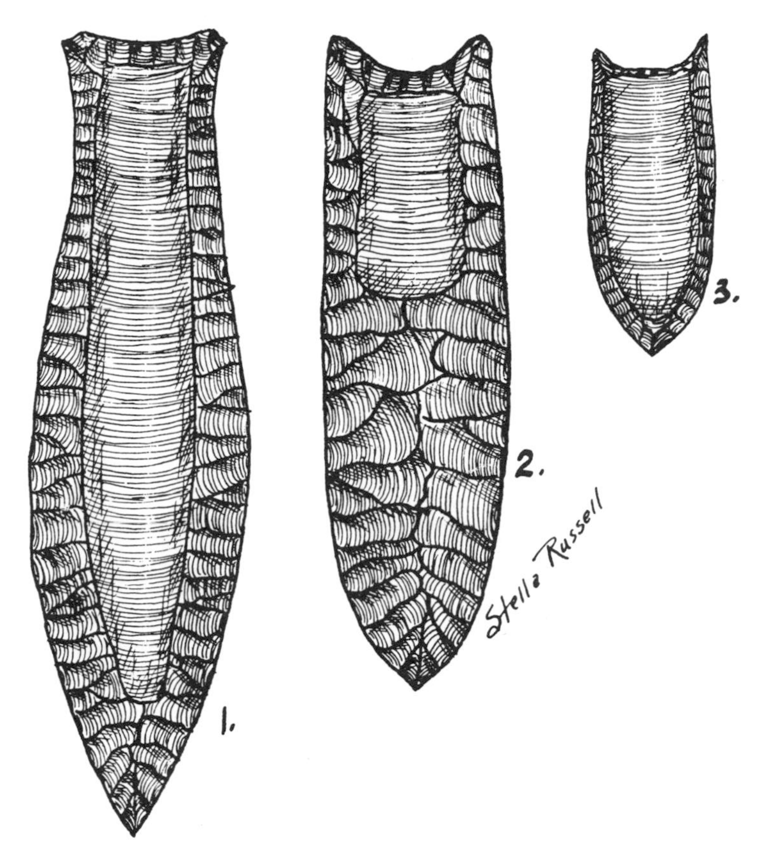

1—Fish-tail Folsom owned by Dr. W. W. Arrasmith, Alliance, Nebraska; 2—called Sub-Folsom, Folsomoid, or Folsom-like; 3—True Folsom or Stub Folsom. 2 and 3 in V. Y. Russell Collection.

is very popular in the west and its popularity is spreading rapidly to all parts of the country. This point is one of the oldest artifacts found in North America, if not the oldest. Like the Yuma, it has not been known very long. The first discovery was made in 1926 near Folsom, New Mexico by a party from the Colorado Museum of Natural History in Denver.

The typical Folsom has a concave base with ear-like projections and a longitudinal flute running down the center of the point. This groove or channel is usually on both faces and runs from one third to the entire length of the point. This groove makes it easy to recognize the point—when you once see a specimen or sketch.

The Folsom seems to be typically American. There are no similar points found in the Old World as in the case of the Yuma, where artifacts with similar flaking have been found in Europe and Africa.

There are several types of Folsoms. The "stub" Folsom has been designated as the true Folsom. These are the ones found in the Folsom, New Mexico site, the Lindenmier site, parts of New Mexico, Colorado and Wyoming. There is another grooved point which is found in other parts of North America. They are longer, heavier, coarser in workmanship and resemble a large Yuma with a groove in the center.

Some authorities call these Folsoms, others term them Folsomoid, Folsom-like, Sub-Folsom or Generalized Folsom. Some say that they are not Folsoms, only grooved or fluted points. So the argument goes, but Mr. Average Collector calls anything that is fluted or grooved a Folsom. Personally, I believe that regardless of what authorities say, the name Folsom has become firmly attached to grooved artifacts and that everything with a groove will generally be known as a Folsom.

The age established for this artifact differs from 10,000

to 25,000 years. Most authorities seem to believe that the Folsom is older than the Yuma, though a few believe that the Yuma is the older.

The two states that have the most Folsoms are Colorado and New Mexico. A few very fine, true Folsoms have been found in Wyoming and Montana. The majority of Folsoms are found a number of feet beneath the surface though some surface finds are made. Surface finds do not have the educational value that the others have. It is impossible to tell where a surface find originally came from.

The thing that the majority of people always ask when they see a Folsom is: What is the purpose of the groove? I will give a number of theories but will not endeavor to reach a conclusion.

The theory most frequently advanced is that this groove allowed the blood to flow freely from the wound. This would bring death quicker to the animal and also bleed it better, just as today we cut the throat of many animals when butchering so that they will bleed freely. Folsom man did not have a horse with which to follow his game. He would throw his spear or javelin into the game, which would probably run for some distance unless the point had struck a vital part. Folsom man would then be able to follow his prey—often by the bloody trail. When he came upon the game, the animal would have "bled," as the channel of the Folsom point would allow the blood to flow out.

Some people believe that the removal of this longitudinal flake would remove most of the weight of the point, giving the projectile great speed and distance. The fluting of the classic Folsom so weakened the point that the type was abandoned. The fact that most of the Foisoms found were broken is good proof of this weakness. All later fluted points were stout and thick with narrowed flutes, giving the projectile great speed and distance.

Still another theory is that the shaft was split and the point forced into the split, along the groove of the point. This was bound around, to hold the point very firm. There are probably other theories, but the three mentioned are the ones most frequently advanced.

Other questions are raised in connection with a study of this ancient artifact. How did the designers succeed in driving out or making this long flake? Folsoms have been found with channels one to five inches long. How did Folsom man do it? Did he make the channel first? Or did he first make the point and then drive the channel? If he made the long flake first, did he then work a point around it and try to make a flake on the opposite side after the point was completed? This theory may be supported by the fact that the flutes are usually much longer and better on one side than on the other. Another theory advanced is that the channels must have been put in last, for had they been put in first, the side chips would break more roughly into the flute. The finger can usually be run smoothly down the channel.

If you have a Folsom or Yuma in your collection you are very fortunate. Folsoms are few and far between; fine ones are almost as rare as fine Yumas. See sketches on page 93.

THE CLOVIS POINT

The average collector would term a Clovis point a Folsom, but it differs from the true Folsom in size, length and length of channel. The channel usually goes from a quarter to three-quarters of the length of the point while the original Folsom has a channel running very nearly the full length of the point. The original Folsom site was found near Folsom, New Mexico and the Clovis site is near Clovis, New Mexico. The points were found in association with the mammoth and in some cases with other extinct forms. The base is

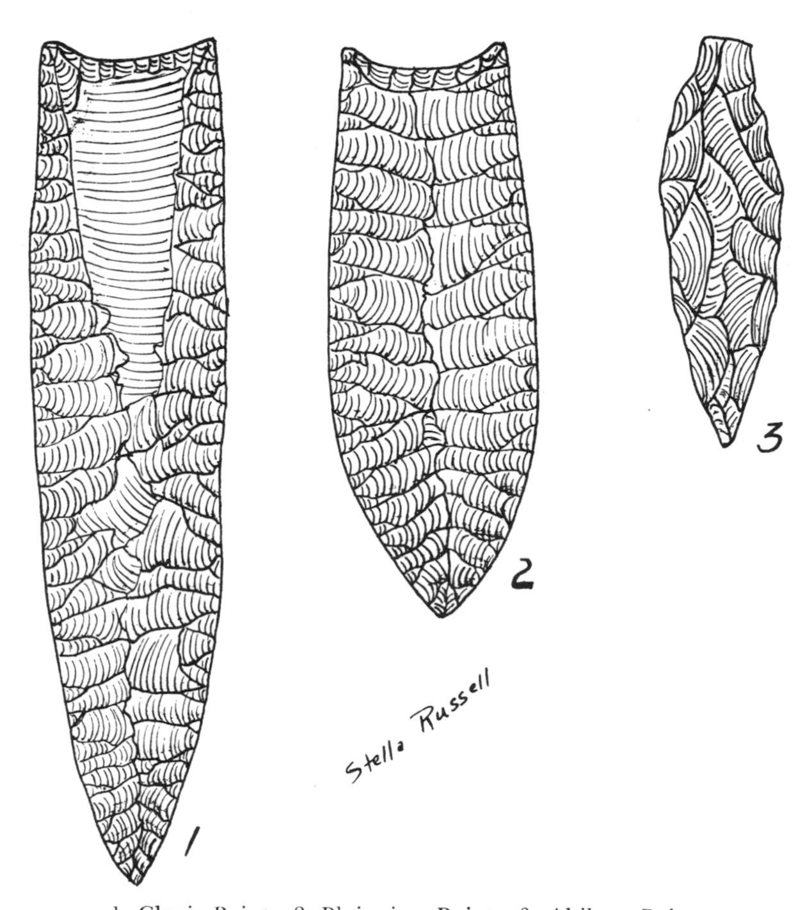

1, Clovis Point; 2, Plainview Point; 3, Abilene Point.

slightly to deeply concave, the cross-section is irregularly bi-concave. They are generally longer than the true Folsom. See sketch on page 97.

MESERVE POINT

According to a letter from E. Mott Davis, Curator of Anthropology at the University of Nebraska State Museum, "The original finds were made near Grand Island, Nebraska, in the 1920's and 30's, associated with *Bison occidentalis*. After that, no more were found in a regular dig until 1950 and 1951, when three were found at the Red Smoke site in the Medicine Creek Reservoir, Frontier County, Nebraska, associated with Plainview points. They have the deep basal concavity and pronounced right-hand bevel. I understand that many specimens of this general type have been found on the surface in some parts of Missouri, where collectors call them "dog-ear" points. I call them Meserve points, after Dr. Meserve who found the first one.

"It is anyone's guess as to whether these are related to the Folsoms or not. At Red Smoke they certainly are found with Plainviews, but not in Missouri. The Red Smoke site may well be as old as the various Folsom sites, but the relationship of Plainview to Folsom or to other types is still unknown."

The Meserve point is illustrated on page 135.

THE SANDIA POINT

Previous chapters have discussed the Yuma and Folsom. Each artifact has some authority who will call it the "older." Now, another artifact has been found which has been called the Sandia. It was found in the Sandia mountains in New Mexico, from which it received its name. The claim of

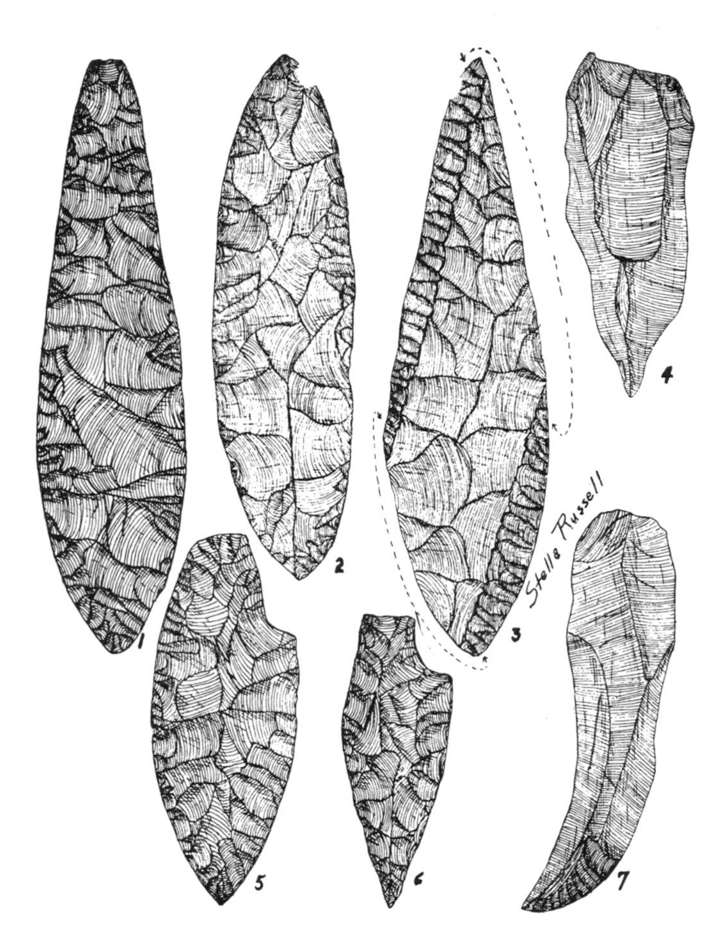

(½ actual size) 1—Black obsidian knife; 2—Flint knife; 3—Four-bevel knife with arrows pointing to bevels on other side; 4—All-purpose tool; 5 and 6—Sandia points; 7—Scalping knife. 3 is owned by Richard Dreher of Topeka, Kansas; 7 is owned by Mr. Starkweather of Casper, Wyoming; others in Walter Jones Collection.

"oldest" rests on the fact that the Sandia artifacts are found on a cultural level below the Folsom; and the Folsom is supposed to be around 25,000 years old. Accordingly, Sandia artifacts may be from 30,000 to 35,000 years old.

The first excavations in a cave in the Sandia mountains uncovered Folsom points; going down deeper, another type of point was found which was later to be known as the Sandia point. The artifacts were found with the remains of camels, sloths and bison. The Sandia point has but one shoulder, which makes it differ from the ordinary point which has two. See page 99 for illustration.

So far, these points are very rare, but as time goes on, others will undoubtedly be found. The first discovery was made in 1935. If the reader thinks that he has a Sandia, he might query the Smithsonian or Dr. Frank C. Hibben at the University of New Mexico, enclosing a drawing or picture, requesting identification of the artifact. Dr. Hibben made the original discovery of the Sandia points. These points have not attracted the average collector as have the Yuma and Folsom; but as time goes on and more are found, they will undoubtedly increase in demand.

CHAPTER 10

VARIOUS INDIAN KNIVES

THE TANG KNIFE

AN Indian artifact known as a tang knife, has sometimes been referred to as a side scraper and a hafted knife. These knives were first found in Texas and at one time it was thought that Texas was the only state in which these artifacts were to be found; but since then, they have been found in Oklahoma, Kansas, Wyoming and possibly in other states.

There are three distinct types of these knives; namely the back tang, the corner tang and base tang. Some of them have a straight cutting edge while others have beveled edges. What is the purpose of these knives? I have been impressed by the fact that they are very rare—as rare as the Folsom and Yuma, if not more so. The widely accepted version is that they were hafted knives, used as scrapers for removing the flesh from hides.

Another theory is that the tang was cut into the knife so that it could be easily carried. The Indian tied a buckskin thong around the tang of the knife and then tied it to his belt so that he could carry a number of such knives without danger of losing them. This does not yet explain the fact that we find so few of them, however. If they were a practical tool, why is it that we do not find more of them? Any Indian who could chip out a spear or knife, could also have made a tang knife so far as ability goes.

The only theory I have ever heard that in any way answers this question, in my mind, is that they were the tool of the medicine man. Another Indian would no more think of making or carrying one of them than a white man would of wearing the pin of a lodge to which he did not belong. He could buy the lodge pin and wear it, but it just isn't done. That might have been the way the Indian felt about the tang knife.

This medicine man story came to me from a man who had spent much time with the Indians and claimed to have been adopted into their tribe. He told this story of the use of the tang knife. The medicine man of the tribe would take a young man and cut an incision in the skin underneath his breasts. Then he would suspend the young Indian by means of a rawhide thong tied through these incisions. If he could tear himself lose, he was a brave; if not, he was still just a youth.

Another tribe is said to have made the incisions in the muscles under the shoulder blade. A large pole was tied to the end of the buckskin thong which was drawn through the incisions. The boy was told to run; he must run until he tore the thongs from his flesh. Then he was a brave.

These incisions were made by the medicine man with the tang knife. He also used this artifact to make incisions for treating snake bites.

The majority of readers can count on the fingers of both hands, if not on one hand, all the good tang knives they have ever seen. I might add that the finest tang knives I have ever seen have been found in Natrona County, Wyoming, in the past few years. They are usually of very fine material with delicate chipping and beautiful lines. See illustration on page 103.

THE FOUR BEVEL KNIFE

The four bevel knife has four distinct cutting blades.

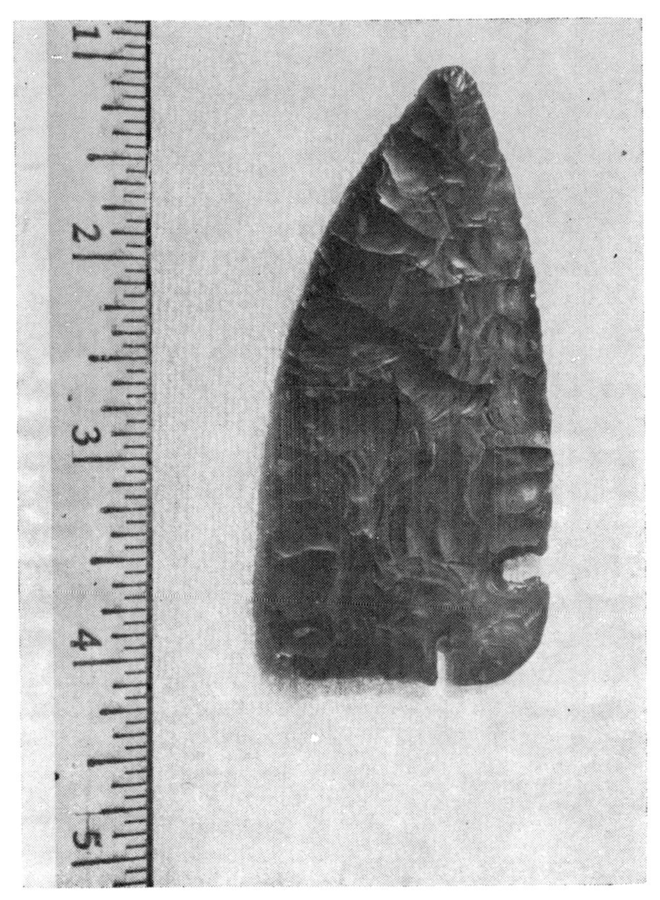

The pride of the Sandison Collection. This beautiful corner tang knife is owned by Tom Sandison of Casper, Wyoming, and was found in the basin of the back waters of Pathfinder Dam in 1939. The knife is of red agate material and is semi-translucent. Several authorities consider this the finest tang knife ever found. A collector may hunt a lifetime but only once in this lifetime does he find a gem like this!

They give the artifact the appearance of being twisted. Some collectors call them four bevel knives and some call them diamond-shaped knives.

These knives are unusual in that they could have been used either by a right or left-handed person. They are considered one of the finest skinning tools known. The workmanship is very fine and they are highly prized by collectors. Some of the bevels have sharp edges, while others have a dull edge. It is truly four knives in one and was used for working skins and hides of different textures. Illustration is on page 99.

THE SCALPING KNIFE

A scalping knife was a long, thin, curved piece of chipped flint, with a sharp edge. The blade was shaped so that it followed the contour of the skull. When the Indian over-powered his enemy, he grasped the hair firmly in one hand and cut around the base of the skull to obtain the "scalp" of his enemy.

Some scalping knives were hafted in hollow horn or bone handles. They were not as common as the regular knife and probably were used only when the Indian was on the war path. Illustrated on page 99.

CHAPTER 11

HAND TOOLS AND HAFTED TOOLS

ELK HORN SCRAPERS

ELK horn scrapers are long, straight pieces of elk horn with a right angle bend on one end. The horn was rubbed sharp upon sandstone. Great pressure could be applied to this scraper and it could be worked more rapidly and with greater ease than the regular stone scrapers. Some believe that a flnt or sharp stone blade was fastened to the end of the scraper. The elk horn was probably placed in hot water until is became soft enough to make the bend in it. A photograph appears on page 143.

THE SCRAPER, FLESHER, KNIFE AND BLADE

Scraper, flesher, knife and blade are terms which have been given to various artifacts and it is sometimes difficult to differentiate between them. Some curators and collectors say there is no difference, because they were all used for the same work. It is true that in many instances each of the artifacts in question could be used in various ways but, technically there is some difference.

The scraper has a rounded, sharp, thin cutting edge. It was used in skinning and in removing the larger pieces of flesh from the skins.

The flesher has a beveled edge and was used for the final dressing of the skin. It was a follow-up tool to remove the last bit of flesh from the skin.

The knife was frequently hafted with bone or wood. It was used in the hand either with leather covering or without. It was primarily a fighting tool, whereas the scraper and flesher were not. It frequently resembles a spear; many so-called spears were used as knives. The knife shows better workmanship than the above mentioned artifacts.

The blade is more of a weapon than an implement. It is frequently only a sharp piece of flint, broken from a core of rock, having very little chipping on it. A blade might be a blank knife. That is, it could easily be worked into a knife.

Roughly, the scraper and flesher were tools for working hides and skins, while the knives and blades were primarily fighting artifacts, which were also used for working skins and other hand work.

THUMB SCRAPERS

Thumb scrapers are very small, well-worked artifacts which are familiar to every collector. They are very common and are not much in demand as far as collectors go. They were used to scrape the meat off the hides of valuable furs.

There are some people who insist they were not scrapers, but spoons. They say they were used to take the marrow out of bones. If one will examine them closely, it will be seen that some of them could have been used for that purpose, especially the long, slender ones. Others argue they were fire stones, used to strike on flint and thereby to start fires. Surely such a tool would be in great demand.

Still others believe they were used by the Indians to pull the hair from their faces. While the Indians generally had no whiskers, the members of some tribes had coarse hair on their faces.

Thus, each individual has his opinion in regard to the use of the thumb scrapers. It is my belief that these thumb

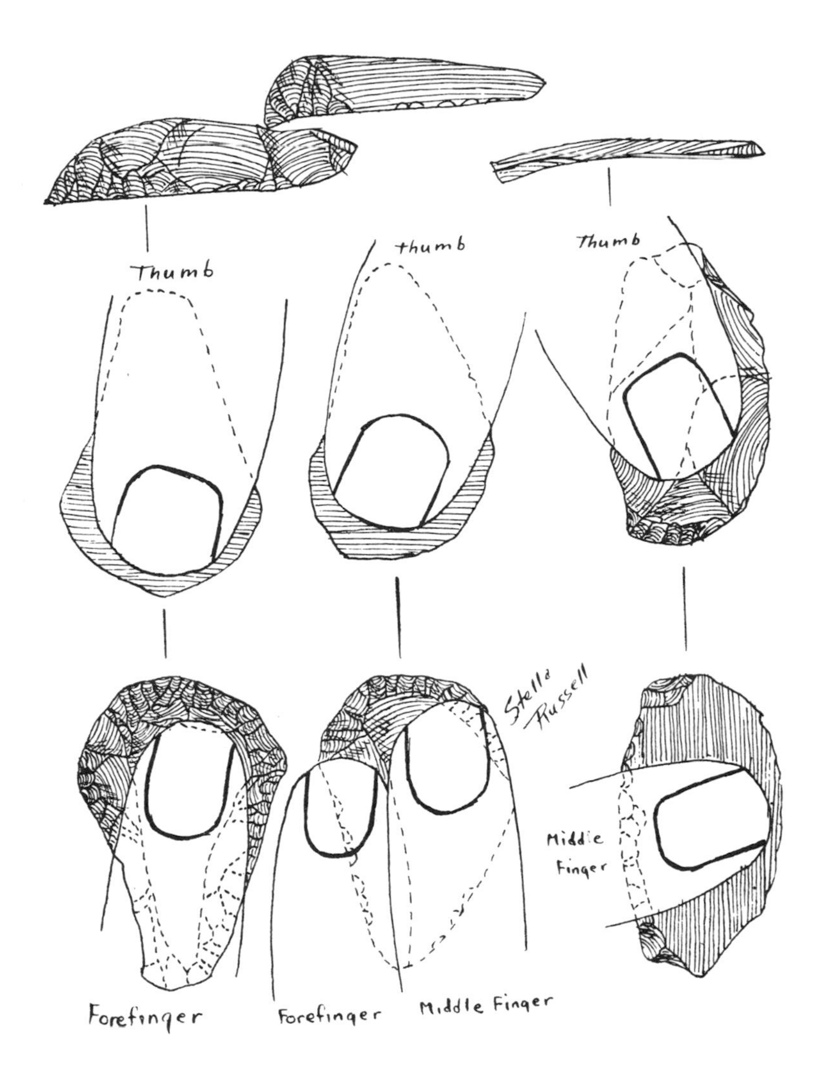

Three thumb scrapers showing the manner in which they are held in the fingers. Top sketches are side views. The one on the right is very thin and may have been used as a fingerknife rather than a scraper.

scrapers, like other tools, were used for various things, but undoubtedly the primary use was as a scraper, to remove the pieces of flesh from the skin. It seems a pity that more interest is not given to these beautiful, well-worked artifacts. I have never found a collector who placed much value on them.

The illustration on page 107 shows three thumb scrapers, illustrating finger holds. (1) This scraper is to be used with thumb and forefinger. (2) This is a three-finger thumb scraper to be used with thumb on the flat side and the forefinger and middle-finger on the raised side. (3) This piece is only one eighth inch thick, with a thin sharp cutting edge. Probably it is a small, finger knife.

THE ALL-PURPOSE TOOL

There are some artifacts that defy all classification. Like some individuals as to nationality, they are a "League of Nations." The tool illustrated on page 99 which was found in Natrona County, Wyoming, is a fair example.

This tool has a sharp point on one end which can be used as an awl, needle or reamer. One edge is quite sharp, like a knife blade. The other edge is flaked and worked down. The end, or hilt, is like that of a chisel. Thus, this piece could be used as an awl, needle, reamer, knife, scraper, chisel, flesher, and, in a pinch, could serve as a spear point.

It is not unusual to find these pieces, nor is it surprising. The wonder is that there were not more of these all-purpose tools. The Indian travelled fast, far, and frequently. He had to travel "light," so it was necessary for him to choose with care the weapons and tools he did carry with him.

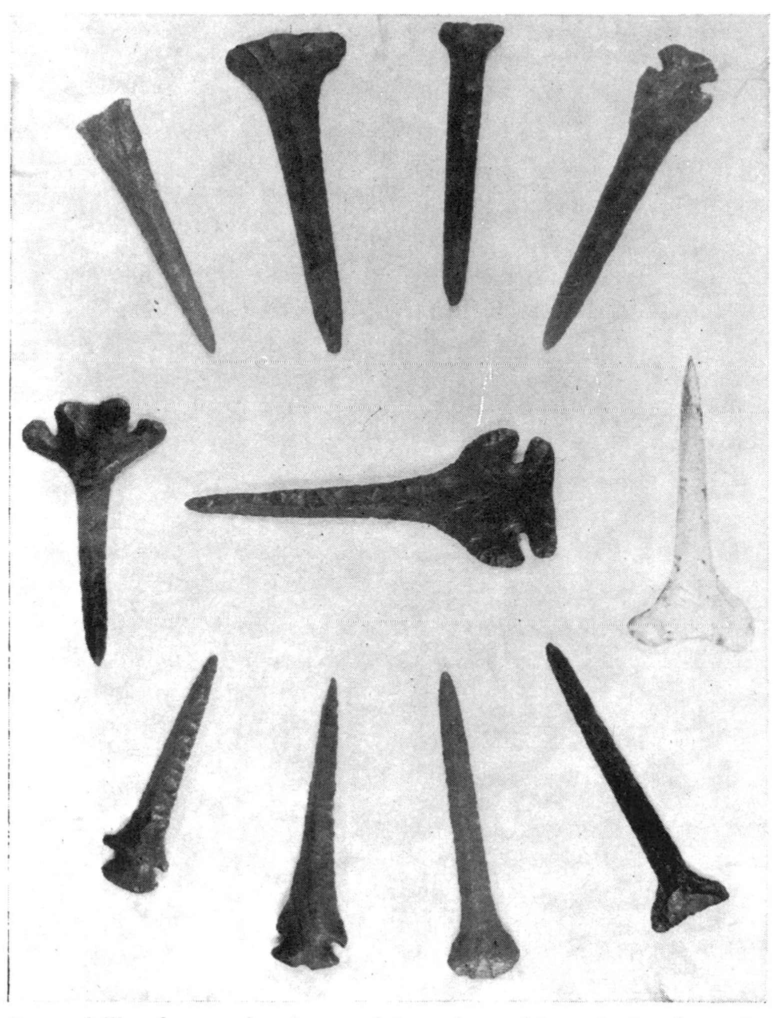

Super drills of exceptional material, workmanship and size, from the States of Ohio, Indiana, Kentucky and Illinois. From Earl C. Townsend, Jr., collection. This cut courtesy Central States Archaeological Journal, Volume 1, Number 3.

THE DRILL

The drill varies in length from two to eight inches, is a long slender artifact with parallel sides and a sharp point. The hilt is blunt and usually forms a "T," so that it can be placed in the hand for a firm hold when pressure is applied. The majority of drills were used to make holes in buckskin or other thick hides that were being made into heavy clothing or tents. Some were used to drill holes in pipes. It is rather difficult sometimes to distinguish between the drill and the awl. An illustration of the drill appears on page 109.

THE AWL OR PUNCH

The awl or punch is not as delicately made or as smoothly flaked as the drill. The drill is long and slender, with parallel sides; the awl is usually tapered to a point, often more like a triangle. The awl was used only in the working of hides and skins and never in the making of pipe stems, though it could have been used in the making of the pipe bowl. The awl is shown on pages 41 and 137.

THE NEEDLE

The needle is long, slender and very delicate as compared to the drill and awl. It was used for finer workmanship than the other two tools, being used in making clothing, moccasins, and other articles made from lighter weight skins. It is very unusual to find a complete needle, as they broke easily and therefore the collector often finds only broken pieces. However, it is not unusual to find many broken needles.

Top, probably the finest flaked celt ever made, found at Mandan, North Dakota; both sides are shown in the picture, it is 2 inches wide, 5½ inches long and ⅞ inch thick through the thickest part; bottom row, general purpose tool, hand axe made of jade, and moccasin last. Celt, M. P. Mosbrucker collection, moccasin last, E. C. Swallow collection.

MOCCASIN LASTS

Stones are found that are about the exact shape of many of our modern shoe lasts. They are found in various sizes, just as people's feet differ in size. The Indians used them to help size their moccasins. The use of these stones in making moccasins was not very common. Hence, few of them are found. But just as our workmen today use various methods, so the Indian undoubtedly made his moccasins in several different ways. Illustration will be found on page 111.

THE SHAFT STRAIGHTENER AND POLISHER

The woods most commonly used in making arrow shafts were ash, birch, willow and wild cherry. The shafts were of no uniform size, length or diameter; the preference of the individual Indian being the determining factor. Sticks were selected that were free from knots; they were straight and smooth. They were cut into proper lengths and hung up to dry for some time. The Indian frequently smoked them during this process.

When the shafts had been seasoned, they were scraped, straightened and polished. When a crook or curve was found on the shaft, it was greased and heated: then it was straightened and put into a stone arrow straightener and allowed to cool. The shaft straightener was a long straight, groove made along one side of an elongated rock, as illustrated on page 141. After the shaft was straightened, it was drawn back and forth along the groove until it became the exact size and roundness of the groove, and acquired a good polish. These grooves were made with the greatest care and were very accurate. Not many of these artifacts were made; yet, I have seen several. They were very practical in making a straight, well-balanced shaft.

BROKEN ARTIFACTS. Preserve them; they are not as valuable as the complete specimens, but may be used for various projects. See pages 50 and 52.

Metate and mano which were found in 1934 by Mrs. R. B. Ravenscroft, Liberal, Kansas.

Some believe that stone rings were used as polishers. By drawing the shaft back and forth through the hole, the shaft was polished by friction.

THE MANO AND METATE

The mano and metate were the two stones or artifacts that the Indian used when grinding his meal. The smaller one, the one held in the hand, was called the "mano" or grinding stone. Camp sites are literally covered with them. The larger stone, into which the grain was poured to be ground, was known as the "metate." These are rarer than the mano and are seldom found in collections. They were much more difficult to make and also to carry around, so that when the Indian left his campsite, he turned the metate over and then they resembled an ordinary boulder. They were heavy to move, often weighing as much as 50 pounds. When they are found they present a problem in transportation. It is said that the Indian turned them over so that the water would not collect in the "bowl" and freeze, cracking the metate. When the Indians returned to this campsite, all they had to do was turn the metate over and it was ready for use.

Wyoming and Colorado campsites have hundreds of the manos and many metates. The metates are valued by collectors, but the manos are so numerous that they have little value. A small mano makes a splendid paperweight and as such makes a suitable gift to send to a friend in some other part of the country. Many people use them in building fireplaces or stone decorations in their dens and playrooms. The larger mano may be utilized as doorstops. Both of these artifacts will become rarer and more valuable as time goes on, since collectors are so careless with them and make little attempt to preserve them. See photo on page 113.

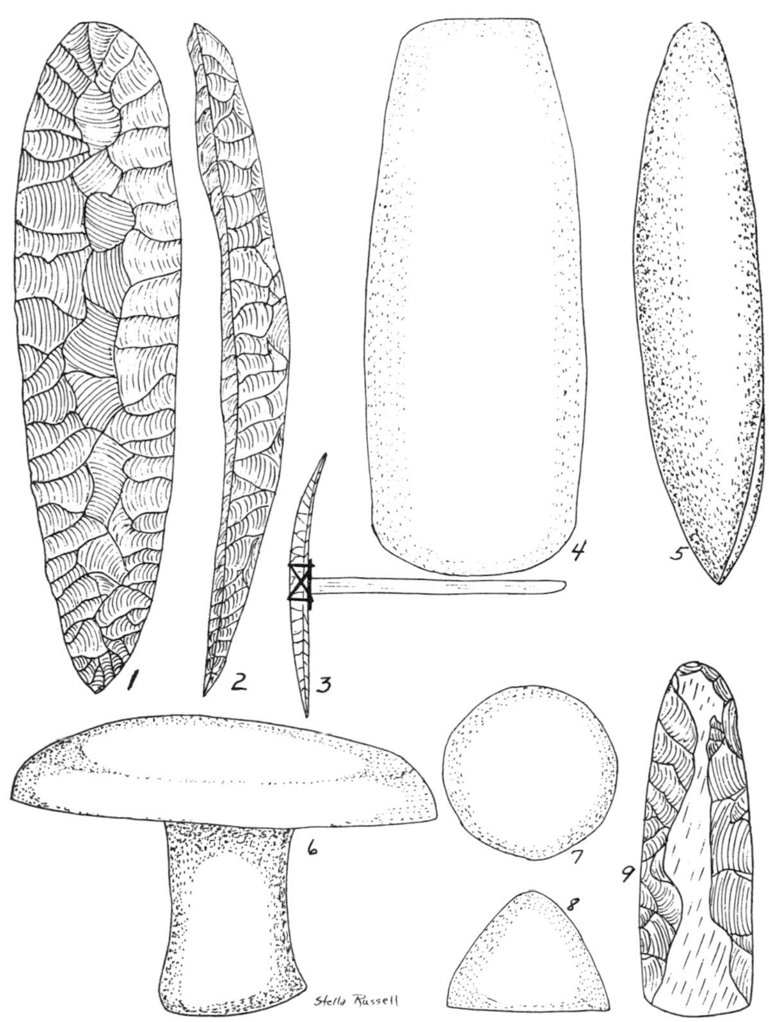

1 and 2, Front and edge views of flint pick, which was probably mounted as in figure 3 and used as a digging tool; 4 and 5, front and side views of a granite adze, being rounded on one side and slightly concave on the other with semi-circular cutting edge; 6, pottery trowel, used in plastering walls of houses with clay in the Mississippi Culture and used in pottery making, it is shaped like a toad stool and rounded on top; 7 and 8, cone of granite, often found made of hematite, polished and probably used as a ceremonial piece or a charm stone; 9, flint chisel, flaked to shape and then the faces and larger end were ground to a sharp edge and polished, probably used as a wedge in splitting wood or as a skinning wedge. All artifacts sketched from material furnished by Edward Zimmerman of Bonne Terre, Missouri.

THE PESTLE

The pestle was used for making meal of various kinds. The grain was placed on a hard surface; then the Indian used the pestle to crack the grain and to pound and roll it into meal and flour. See photo on page 77.

CHISELS

Chisels are long, slender stone tools with the edge sharpened like a modern day chisel. Since the upper end is seldom round and blunt, it shows they were not struck with a heavy stone hammer as we hit our own chisels today. The power was applied with pressure, not by striking. The material from which they are made couldn't stand to take the rough usage that our iron chisels do today. Chisels are chipped and also made by grinding stones into polished chisels. See illustration on page 115.

SPATULATES OR SPUDS

The spatulate, or spud, is a type of flared celt. It is ground and polished like a celt but flares out at the base and has a rather long, slender handle. There are numerous theories as to the use of the spatulate, they may be divided into two general divisions. One is ceremonial and the other utilitarian. It seems to me that both schools of thought could be correct. The highly polished spatulates with outstanding workmanship were used as ceremonials, while the ordinary and more common specimens were for utility purposes. The utility use varied such as to remove bark from trees, dress hides, make dug-out canoes, skinning large animals and many other uses that a chisel-like instrument could perform. However, undoubtedly those with long, delicate handles, mirror-

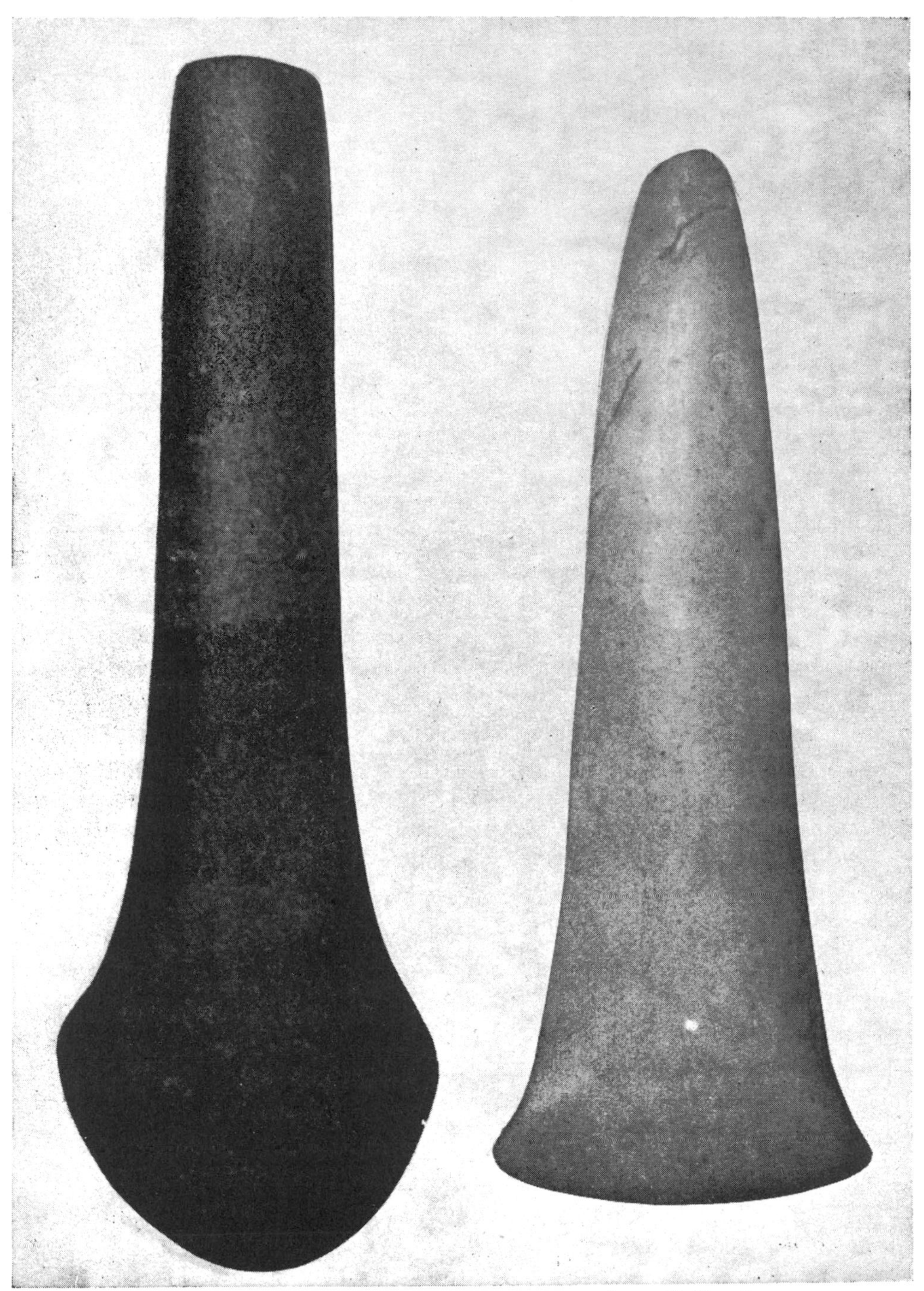

Spatulates. Left, black and white wirery granite from Shelby County, Illinois, length 10¾ inches. Right, cream color flint, ground and polished, from Humphreys County, Tennessee, length 9½ inches. From Byron Knoblock collection. This cut courtesy Central States Archaeological Journal, Volume 1, Number 2.

like polish and showing no evidence of having been in active use were probably used as ceremonials. See illustration on page 117.

CONES

Cones derive their name from their shape. The base is usually flat and they vary in thickness from those that are nearly flat to those that are thicker than their diameter. They are usually made from hematite and polished. They were probably used as ceremonial pieces or as charm stones. See illustrated on page 115.

GOUGES

Gouges have a curved cutting edge, and one side is hol lowed out. The hollowed-out portion usually runs from one-third to two-thirds of the length of the gouge but sometimes will run the full length. They may have been used with a hammer or maul as indicated by the badly battered heads on many specimens. They were thought to have been used to tap maple sugar trees in some areas or to remove wood from the inside of logs that were to be used to make dug-out canoes, or to peel bark from tree trunks. An illustration will be found on page 119.

NOTES ON HAFTING OF STONE TOOLS

By M. W. Hill, Alexandria, Virginia

The beginning of hafting was probably the first great step of primitive man in his rise out of the animal state in the dim past. Work was accomplished by use of sharp edges of whatever material was most easily obtained and could be held in the hand but such tools were hard on the hands and slow to work with. The many types of stone artifacts found

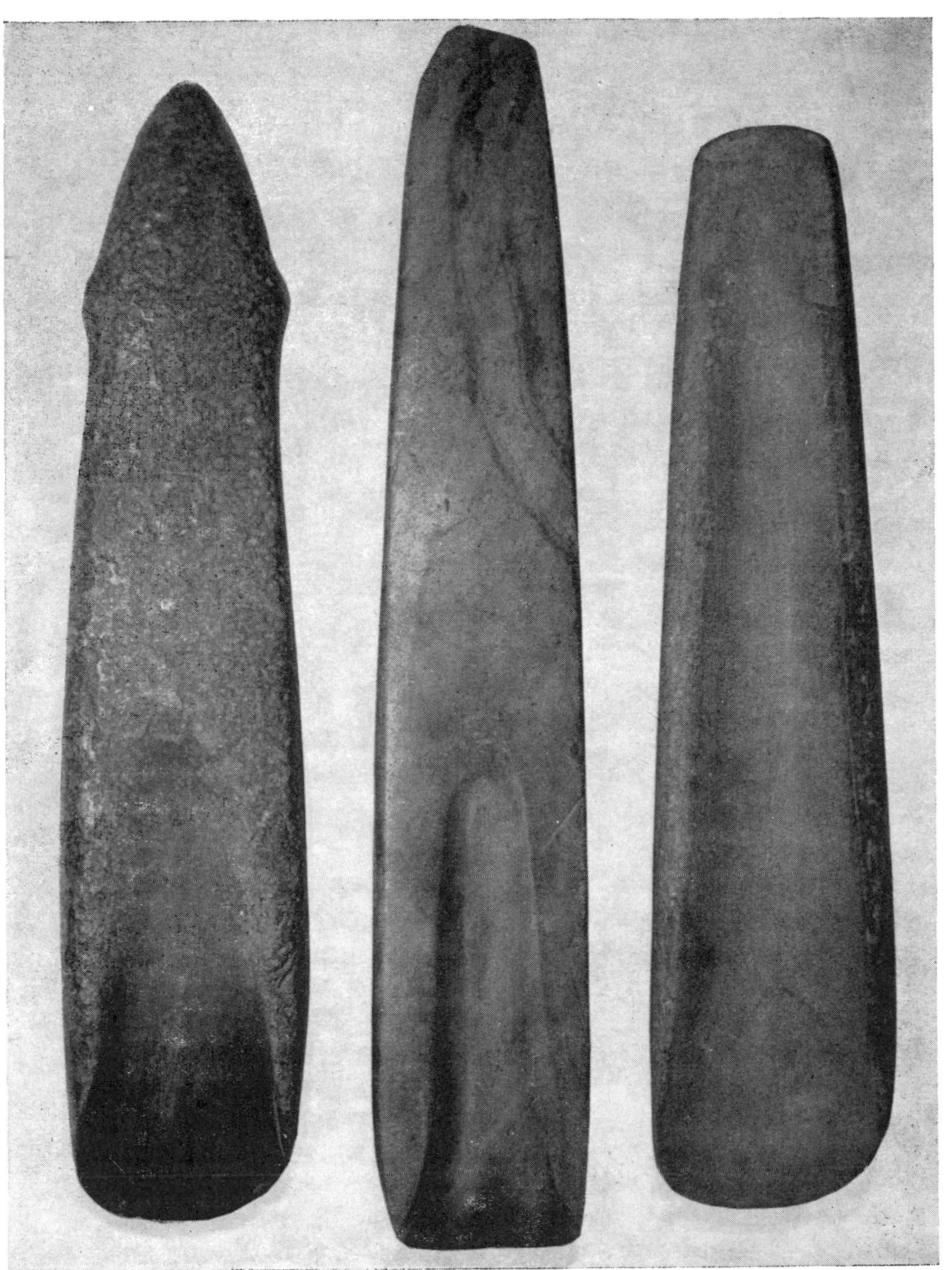

Grooved gouges. Left: Knobbed or effigy gouge from St. Lawrence County, New York. Material black granite. Length 9½ inches. Center: A beautiful gouge from Crittenden County, Virginia. Material greenstone. Length, 10 inches, cross section triangular. Right: Gouge from Oswego County, New York. Material plain gray granite. Length 9¼ inches. From B. W. Stephens collection. This cut courtesy Central States Archaeological Journal, Volume 2, Number 4.

with stems as aids to fastening prove that hafting was common practice the world over.

My theories are based upon the fact that most of the American Indians were migrants and few stayed all the year round in one place. They travelled light and long hafted tools would be left behind or only the stone blade would be carried along. Hafting was of three kinds in general: hasty, semi-permanent and, with sedentary tribes, permanent. I think 90% of all hafting was hasty, being done for one job or for use for a short time only.

The form of haft for a given shaped stone was doubtless one of those things discovered by the old trial and error method but in time the best and easiest types of hafts were developed. Study brought out the advantage of utilizing natural form and shape in the wood from which the haft was cut so a minimum of alteration was required. Hollow material such as bone, horn and plants like cane, bamboo and other pithy growths were sought out as they saved the time to drill sockets. The use of prongs and stubs of branches afforded good anchors for lashings.

It is well to remember that large areas have no forests and such wood as is found is drift brought down by flood waters. Under such conditions an inadequate handle may be due to the lack of more suitable material or probably more often to lack of time. Bone, however, will be found wherever man exists and was used whenever suitable for the purpose wanted. Tools mounted at an angle to the main axis of the haft were often lashed to a stub limb extending from the stick at the desired angle. The hoe, a very common tool, was usually mounted in this fashion.

To avoid excess weight in the handle, large thick tools that were too big to mount in the prong without unduly weakening it in hollowing the sides to fit the groove in the stone should best be lashed with the use of splints lashed to the handle, and extending over the sides of the stone tool and permitting a strong friction grip holding the stone in place. It is unlikely that long handled and heavy tools were carried along when a tribe moved into a new area but were hidden or cached until the tribe returned once more.

In every hafting a sensible relationship between the haft and the stone tool must be maintained if the tool is to have any life. Any edged tool will suffer damage when the haft is too big or too long and lashed too tight as these conditions are an invitation for abuse and not proper use. Relashing or tightening is a matter of minutes, the sharpening of any fine tool is a tedious process.

A factor of safety can be provided through the lashings which for a heavy tool will have to be tight but for the small, lighter weight tools, the ties may be light and not too tight, so that the lashings will work loose if the tool is subjected to stresses that it is not designed for. It is far better to relash than to damage the tool's edge.

Many spalls struck from fine grained flint have a sharpness almost equal to a steel razor and these when used mounted as a tool must be handled with the same delicacy as a razor. A precision-made example will be found occasionally of almost every type of stone tool, the product of a master worker. No doubt these fine tools were hafted with more than the ordinary care and with the best of material for lashings. Many different techniques were doubtless used by men with different manual skills and used for just ordinary projects or those in which more thought and care were necessary.

The materials for hafting were varied, gut and rawhide probably being the best of all as they shrink upon drying. Vines, inside barks and many grasses have tough fibres and are flexible so can be wound tight without breaking and it is most probable that the majority of hafting was done with the material that was at hand.

Rawhide, sinew and gut are about the best lashing materials but were not always available and so others were desirable. Thread-like fibres were necessary for all very small hafting jobs and were obtained from hair, Yucca and similar vegetable growths. The inside bark of many trees can be divided into fine fibres when the bark is green. I have used privet, maple and N.C. poplar all of which gave strong, fine flexible lashings. The use of small removable wedges was a quick way to tighten any set of lashings. When asphalt or gums were at hand their use to hold the lashings in place were found effective, also to help in waterproofing the hafting. Evidence of the use of adhesives is present upon quite a number of artifacts in every collection.

The processing of skins, large and small, required many tools and much labor with the hands and even the teeth in softening the skins for garments. Delicate bird and fish skins required special techniques. Furs and feathers being one of the most common of decorative material required special curing processes and special tools during these manipulations. The American Indian also had certain surgical skills as is in evidence by bone growth shown upon skeletal remains showing an operation which was successful. Delicate tools requiring equally delicate hafting were undoubtedly necessary to carry out these tasks.

Finally, after re-flaking several hundred damaged arrow heads, I have a very strong hunch that many stone workers had some hafted tools in their kit and did not altogether rely upon the wood or bone flaker. Such master-craftsmen as those who produced the machine-like flaking visible on some Folsom and Yuma type blades, I believe had some auxiliary aids in their kits beside the flaker.

Summarizing, the necessities of life may not have depended upon hafting but I am safe in saying the real comforts of life did.

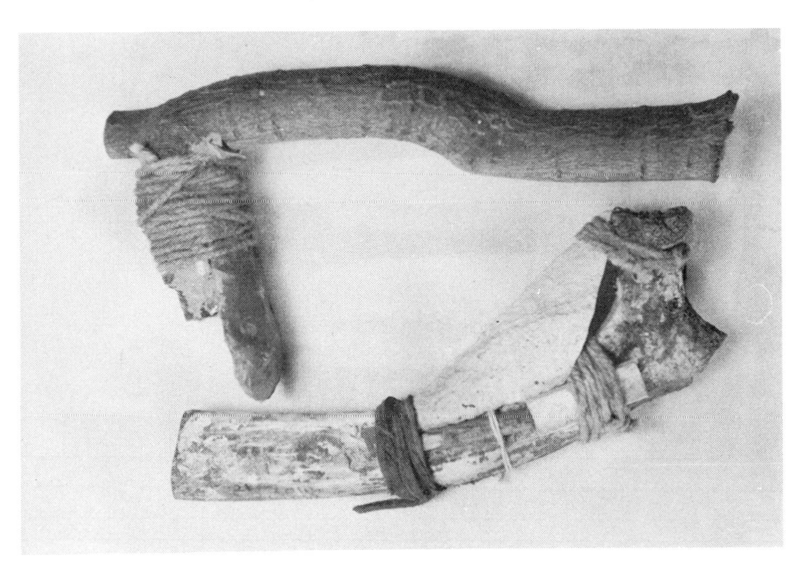

Fine examples of hafting on wood and on bone. These specimens were very capably mounted by M. W. Hill of Alexandria, Virginia to show methods used for hafting artifacts. Mr. Hill is probably the outstanding authority on hafting of artifacts.

CHAPTER 12

PROJECTILE POINTS

BIRD POINTS

THE small arrowheads found in various parts of the country are called bird points. It would be impossible to state that all points up to a certain size are bird points, but the majority of collectors seem to agree that they may be up to three quarters of an inch in length. Some claim they may be up to one inch in length. Bird points usually show the most delicate workmanship of any of the Indian artifacts. The hilts are of so many various shapes that it would be impossible to state how many different hilts there might be. Page 137 shows illustrations of some of the more common hilts.

The name bird point has been given to these small arrowheads because many believe they were used on arrow shafts to shoot small game, especially birds. If the Indian did hunt birds, they would undoubtedly have used a very small point, for a larger one would have destroyed too much of the bird.

There are those who contend that these small points were used to kill large game as well as birds. They state that the small sharp piece of flint on the end of an arrow shaft would go in easier and penetrate farther than a large projectile. Some say that these points were used to train the Indian children to hunt, noting that today we give our children toy guns and pistols.

Another theory is that there were tribes of small Indians

or "Pygmies" who used these small arrowheads; almost every section of the country has its legend of little men. Wyoming has a legend of the *sheep eaters* who were supposed to be dwarfs; the Southeast has its legend of the Little Men of the Cumberland Mountains.

Most authorities, however, believe that bird points were used to kill birds and small game.

THE SPEAR POINT

The best known and most common Indian projectile point, next to the arrowhead, is the spear point. The spear might be termed a "grown-up"arrow. Some authorities say that a spear is any projectile point over two inches long, while others say that they are three inches and longer. The spear is one of the most popular of all Indian artifacts. It will not sell for as much as some other pieces, but it has a popularity with all collectors that is not exceeded by any other artifact.

Good spears are getting scarcer all the time. They are so much larger than other arrows that they are easier to find. They are not as common as the arrow point. Many artifacts called spears are in reality knives or blades, but as one authority said, "It is impossible to draw a definite line between the various artifacts. Today, we use pliers, for instance, for various kinds of work. The same need was much more prevalent in the past. An Indian might use a stone artifact as a knife; later, needing a spear, the same knife might serve his purpose."

Mr. W. W. Hill of Alexandria, Virginia, writes:

"Webster says a spear is a long pointed weapon used in war and hunting by thrusting or throwing as a lance. To think of a spear of being thrown as a missile is a misconception of the weapon. That spears and lances were sometimes

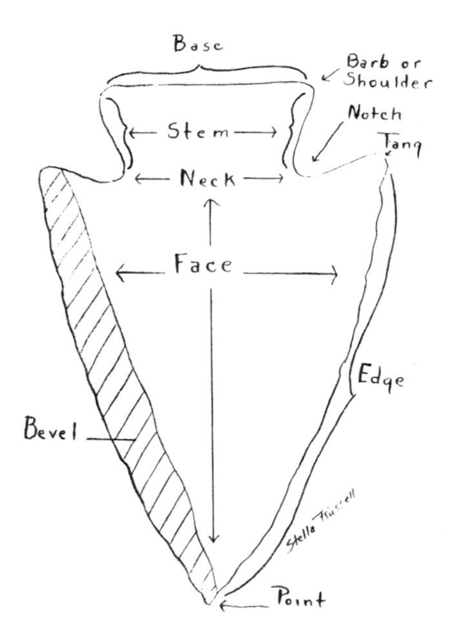

This drawing identifies the various parts of an arrowhead. The collector may also make a study as to the kind of material; the age of the projectile; the tribe that made it; the kind of chipping it has; and its possible use Was it a war, hunting or poison point? Is it an arrowhead or a spear point? What is the commercial value of the point? Is it authentic, modern or fake? Would a collector or museum want it? Was it a surface or depth find? If a depth find, what depth? Were there any bones found with it? If so, what kind of bones? Does it show signs of patina? Does it have sand scratches? Is it the type of artifact frequently found in that locality or is it a point which is foreign to that location?

Thus, one could go on and on, studying and pondering over this triangular bit of stone.

thrown by the user was doubtless true, but only as a last resort.

"When the spearman loses his grasp on his spear he is partially unarmed as the spear's length was his greatest protection. The spear to be effective must be a stout, strong weapon designed to stand hard use with sufficient length to keep the enemy at such a distance that his shorter weapons are ineffective.

"The spear must not be so heavy as to prevent easy and swift movement in any direction by the user. It is logical therefore, to consider the spear as a thrusting weapon only.

"The javelin or Pilum of the Romans was a shorter weapon about 60 inches in length, sufficiently light to be thrown a good distance with velocity sufficient to kill the quarry. This type of projectile was small and light enough so that a number of reserves could always be carried by the hunter. It is likely that when the flint spear heads were suitably thin, they may have been hafted upon javelins."

How were the spears hafted? A number of methods were used. They were secured to the shaft by buckskin thongs, by plant fiber, and by various gums from trees and vegetation. There are many kinds of spears. I will not attempt to name all of them but some are called side-notch, bevel, oak-leaf, willow-leaf, dove-tail, turkey-tail, beaver-tail, Yuma, Folsom, serrated, steel and ceremonial spears. Illustrations may be found on page 129 and 155.

BEVELED POINTS

Beveled points are spears with beveled edges, as the name indicates. They are divided into two groups, left and right hand bevels. Whether it is a left or right bevel depends on whether the Indian who made it was left or right handed.

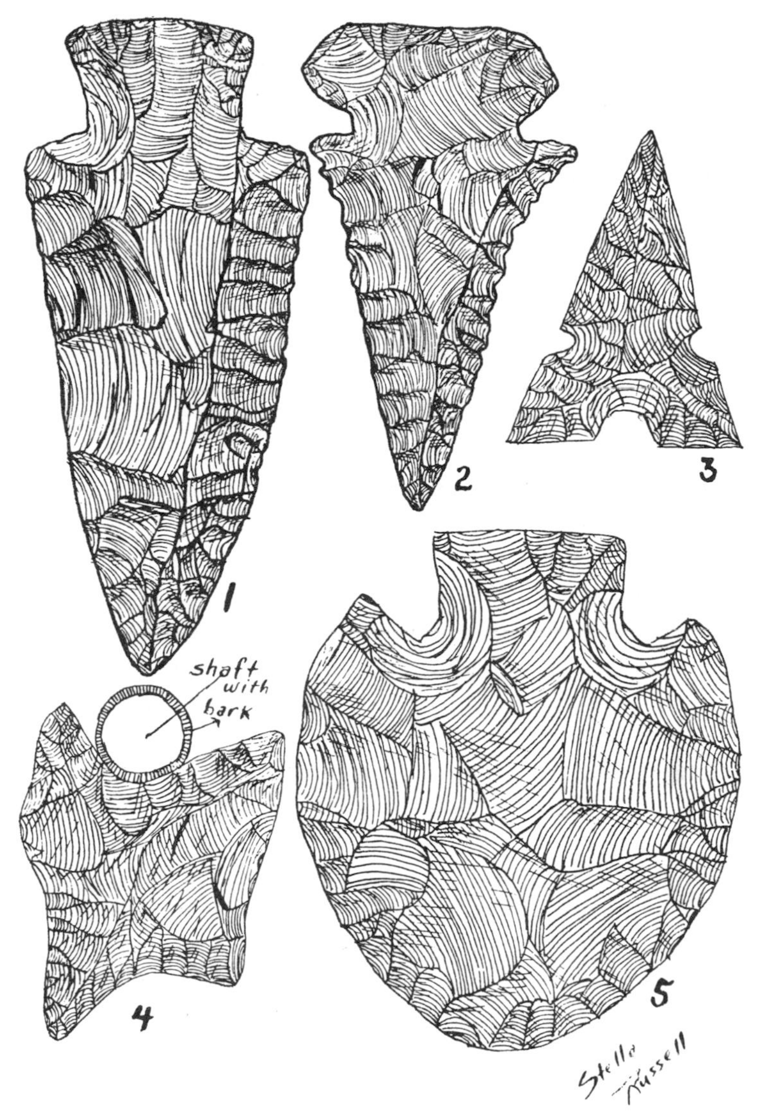

1 and 2 are spears with beveled edges. 3—Three-point arrow. 4—Shaft scraper with sketch of shaft, with possible awl on opposite corner. 5—Large stunner. Walter Jones Collection.

Many Indians were left handed, as can be determined by their artifacts.

The beveled edge gave the arrow a whirling motion in flight. The beveled point could also be used as a knife or scraper. These points are not common, though they are not as rare as some other types of spears, such as the dove-tail or turkey-tail spears. Illustrations appear on page 129.

STUNNERS

The stunner was a large, blunt projectile used to stun, cripple or kill the game without having the artifact penetrate the body. Stone artifacts were difficult to make; a great deal of time and effort was expended in their making. The Indian had to be economical in the use of his hunting artifacts. Many times an arrowhead or spear was much more valuable than the game at which it was shot. It seldom brought instant death; this permitted the animal to proceed for some distance, and, in many cases, the animal was successful in escaping altogether.

So, the Indian conceived the idea of using a dull, blunt artifact that would cripple or stun the animal, but would not enter the body and thus be carried away. If he shot it at a badger, or coyote, the arrow would drop to the ground after striking the game and could easily be found and used again. The stunner was often made from a broken spear or arrow. The broken spear was no longer of value as a spear, but could be re-chipped and used as a stunner. A sketch appears on page 129.

POISON POINTS

There are many conflicting stories regarding the poison point. What shape of point was it, and what method was used in poisoning it? Most collectors I have talked to say it was a triangular shaped point. There was no way to fasten this point to the arrow shaft. The end of the shaft was split, the point was forced into the slit and the arrow was fired. When someone tried to remove the shaft by pulling on it, the point remained in the wound.

Other people claim the poison point was a jagged projectile with saw-tooth, or serrated edges. The poison was put into the serrations; thus a great amount of poison could be injected into the wound. There are those who say that a point of any shape could be used as a poison point, that the poison was placed on them and that the shape did not matter. Another version is that the poison point was made on the principle of a fish hook. It would enter easily, but was almost impossible to pull out.

What kind of poison was used? The poison of reptiles, especially that of the rattlesnake, was often used. Poison was sometimes extracted from certain plants and decaying meat was said to have been used at times. With reference to the rattlesnake poison, the Indians took a piece of fat meat, let the snake bite it many times; then the arrow points were put into the poisoned meat and baked. This method was common when the Indians had steel points which he purchased from the white man. The points were allowed to rust, before they were baked in the poison meat. Thus, the poison penetrated deep into the points.

There are those who claim that the Indian would place a piece of liver on an ant hill and allow the ants to bite it for some time. Then the points were placed into the liver and left there until the liver decayed.

There is very little doubt, in my mind, that the Indian in various parts of the country used different poisons, so it is quite likely also that they used various shaped arrow heads for their poison points. Some triangular points are illustrated on page 91; a serrated point is illustrated on page 147.

METAL POINTS

Metal or iron arrow points were made by both the Indian and the white man. The majority of these metal points were made by fur trading companies and sold or bartered to the Indian for furs. The Indian found them superior to the stone points in most respects; consequently, they were in great demand. The Hudson's Bay Company probably sold the majority of these points to the Indians of the Northwest. The usual value was from one to three cents each, according to the number purchased.

The majority of these points are found all through the Rocky Mountain region, especially in the Northwest. They are of various sizes and shapes, just as the stone artifacts are. The arrows intended for hunting have rounded shoulders and are therefore easily removed from a wound, whereas war points have square shoulders which make them much more difficult to extract.

The machine-made point is much more perfect, often being carefully beveled. The stem is usually serrated or notched to enable the warrior to bind it firmly to the shaft. The Indian frequently made these points from bits of metal taken from harnesses, old wagon boxes or where ever he might find suitable material.

If a metal point is very crude, it was made by the Indian. If it appears precisely cut it was probably a trade arrow, secured from one of the fur trading companies. Some people say that the Indians also bought the material as well as the finished arrows and made the points themselves.

These points are fast disappearing as the iron rusts and decays. The genuine "steels" will soon be a thing of the past.

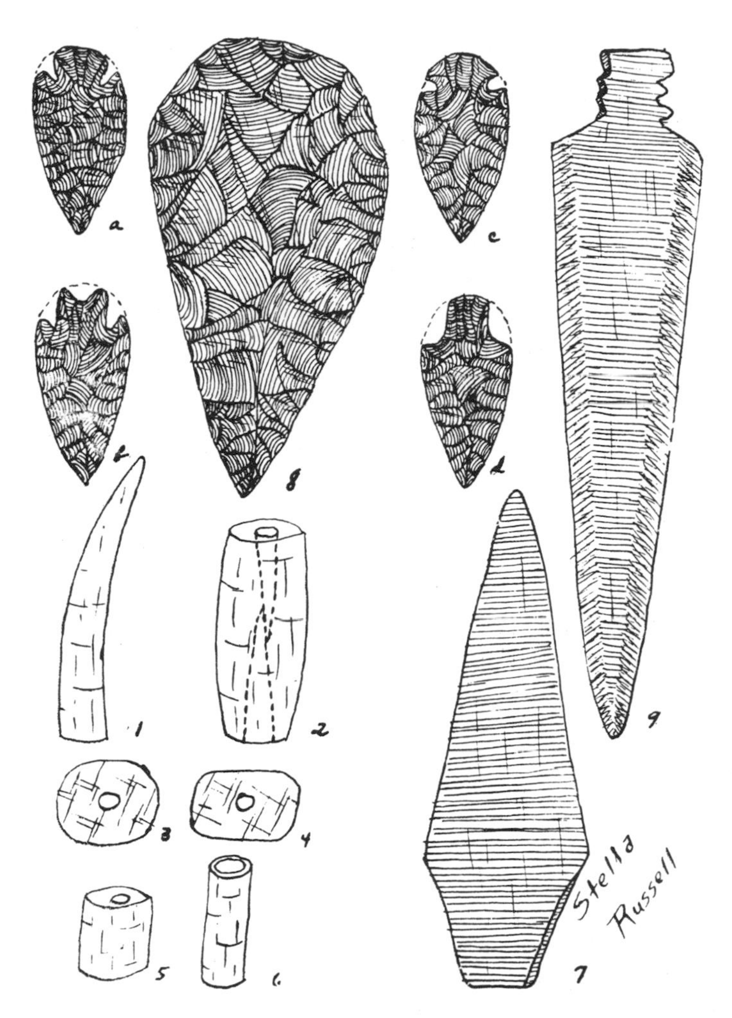

1—Dentallium bead. 2—Barrel-shaped bead showing possible drilling through the bead. 3—Circular shell bead. 4—Rectangular shell bead. 5—Wampum. 6—Bone bead. 7—Steel arrow of the type the Indians made. 9—Steel arrow of the type made by the white man and sold to the Indians. 8—Quarry blank with a,b, c and d showing the various shaped arrows which can be made from the quarry blank.

If you have one, treasure and keep it. Both types of these points are sketched on page 133.

THE QUARRY BLANK

The Indian likes to use various types of material in making his artifacts. When he passed through a part of the country in which suitable material could be found, he carried as much of it with him as possible. Naturally, he could not carry large boulders or rocks, so he worked them down into small pieces. He carried these along to be made into complete pieces when he had time, or as they were needed. He could make any one of ten possible types of arrows from two basic types of quarry blanks.

The Indian heated the rocks of his choice until they were red hot, then threw them into cold water, which would cause them to break. Repeating this from time to time, he finally secured small pieces, suitable for working into arrowheads. The so-called quarry blank was worked from a sliver of stone removed from the larger rock. Quarry blanks are found in various stages of completion. A quarry blank is sketched on page 133.

FRACTURED BASE POINTS

The general contour of this unique type of projectile point is trianguloid. Shallow, diagonal V-shaped notches are worked between the very flat or slightly concave base. The base projects ever so slightly beyond the level of the shoulders, and invariably presents a fractured surface.

This fractured surface has been effected by squarely breaking off the basal material; the technique of this procedure may, or may not, have been quite simple but it is the only example of its kind among Ohio flint projectiles.

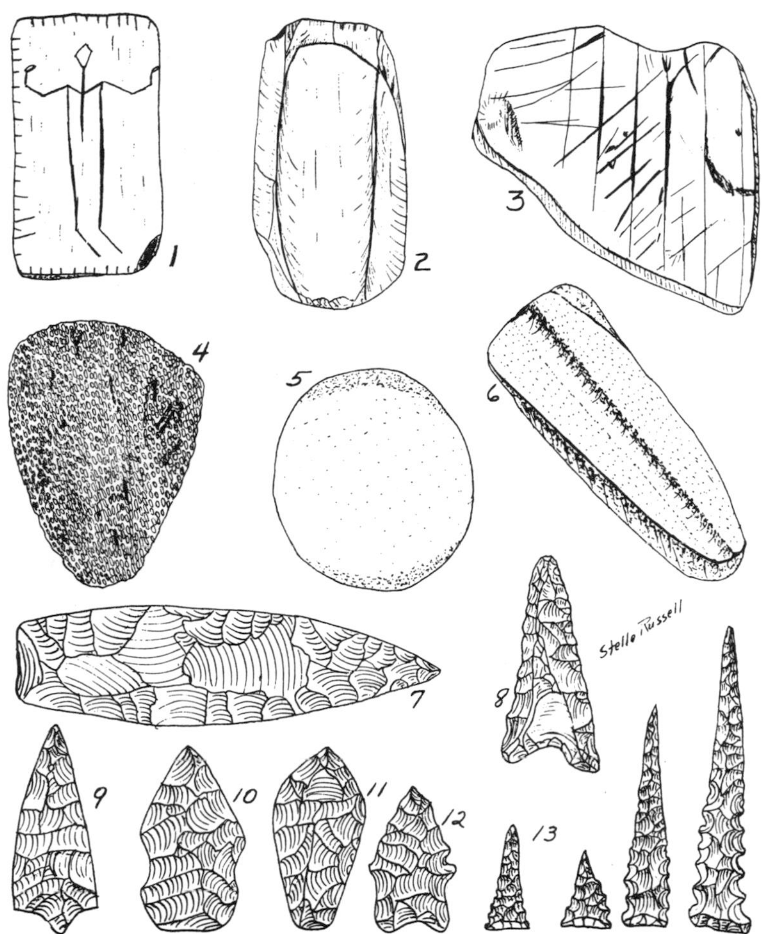

1, Bone game piece made from a deer rib, unsplit, with effigy of human being, line carved, incised on ends and one side—a rare piece; 2, deer bone game piece, made from deer shank bone, with calcellous material removed, it is highly polished and shows no incisions; 3, boulder game piece made from a claylike boulder which probably needed no shaping, nicely incised on one side, shows rubbing on reverse side; 4, buffalo bone abrader made from the knee bone of the bison and highly abrasive, it is hard and shows no sign of the hard wear it must have undergone; 5, hammerstone, shows ample evidence of hammering on both ends, was probably a small, round boulder which was picked up and held in one hand; 6, hone made of pumice stone and used for straightening bone tools and sometimes called an abrader; 7, Lanceolate, typical of an early period in Missouri; 8, Merserve point; 9, Gypsum cave dart point; 10, Silver Lake dart point; 11, Lake Mohave dart point; 12, Pinto Basin dart point; 13, and next three points, various sizes of Hohokam points. 1 through 6, Mandan artifacts courtesy M. P. Mosbrucker, Mandan, North Dakota; 8, courtesy E. Mott Davis, Curator, State Museum, Lincoln, Nebraska; 9 through 12 courtesy M. R. Harrington, Curator, Southwest Museum, Los Angeles 42, California; 13, etc., courtesy E. B. Sayles, Curator, Arizona State Museum, Tucson, Ariz.

It occurs in widely separated collections throughout Ohio and it also occurs in Indiana, Kentucky and possibly elsewhere. Illustrations may be found on page 25.

THE ABILENE POINT

The artifacts known as Abilene Points were first discovered in 1929 by Dr. Cyrus N. Ray in the region of central Texas. Dr. Marie Wormington in ANCIENT MAN IN NORTH AMERICA, describes the Abilene Points: "They are about two or three inches in length, thick, crudely flaked by percussion and roughly leaf-shaped. In some examples flakes have been removed from one side resulting in a stem beveled to the right." Dr. Wormington also states that these finds are dated as being "pre-pottery complexes." They were found at considerable depth below the surface. Sketch may be found on page 97.

THE GYPSUM CAVE POINTS

The Gypsum cave points were found near Las Vegas, Nevada. They were found in a cave known as Gypsum Cave, thus the name. They are almost a perfect triangle in shape except for the concave projection on the base. These points are believed to have been used as dart points. They were found associated with the bones of the ground sloth and the extinct American camel. The age, by carbon 14 test has been determined at 8,000 to 10,000 years. The discovery was made in 1930 by an expedition under Dr. Mark R. Harrington under the supervision of the Southwest Museum of Los Angeles. Illustration appears on page 135.

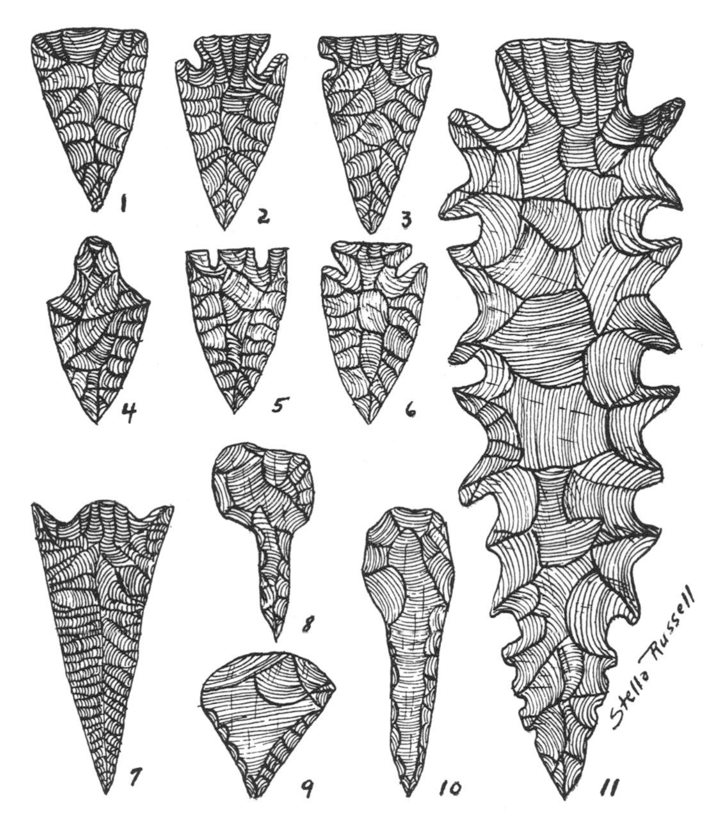

1 through 7 shows various hilts of bird points; 8—drill; 9—awl; 10—drill; 11—ceremonial.

THE PINTO BASIN POINTS

These points were found in the Pinto Basin in southeastern California. The majority of the Pinto Basin points, if not all, were surface finds. The discovery was made by an expedition under the auspices of the Southwest Museum in 1934. They were not found associated with any bones. The point is a stubby, thick, projectile point and was possibly used with the the atlatl instead of the bow and arrow. Most of these points were surface finds along old dry lake beds. These lakes were full of water eight to ten thousand years ago, dried up and then filled again about four thousand years ago. Dr. Harrington says that many archaeologists believe the Pinto Points were connected with the older period. The points are rather crudely made, with slight shoulders and concave bases. Illustrated on page 135.

LAKE MOHAVE POINTS AND SILVER LAKE POINTS

The Lake Mohave and Silver Lake points were discovered under the direction of the Southwest Museum. The discovery was made in the Mohave Desert, about 150 miles from Los Angeles. The discovery brought out two different types of projectile points, probably dart points. The first one was called the Mohave point and its general shape is leaf-like, it is long and tapering, have very slight shoulders and a convex base. The other type, known as the Silver Lake point has a more pronounced base and is less tapering. Most of these points were found on the shores of lake beds which have been dry a long time. The age is estimated to be from four to eight thousand years old. I received this information through the courtesy of Dr. Mark R. Harrington of the Southwest Museum. The Lake Mohave and Silver Lake points are illustrated on page 135.

CHAPTER 13

HEAVY ARTIFACTS

THE AXE OR MAUL

AXES and mauls, or "skull crushers" as they are sometimes called, are of two general types, flaked and polished. The flaked axes are for cutting, having sharp edges and are more of a true ax.

The second group are polished axes or mauls. They are termed one-half groove, three-quarters groove, and full groove, depending on how far the groove was worked around the maul. The name skull crusher is applied because they were used to crush the skull of buffalo in order to obtain the brain. The brain was not only delectable food, but it was also used in tanning hides. Photos appear on pages 51 and 77.

THE HOE

There are three types of hoes. The most common one is the celt type. The other two are the notched hoe and the stemmed hoe. Not many of the hoes are found in the Rocky Mountain region, though some are found which have probably been carried in from the plains regions and other parts of the country where the Indian gave more attention to agriculture. See pages 71, 141 and 143.

THE SPADE

There are four types of spades. The most common type is similar in shape to our modern spade, and is usually referred to as a flare spade. Then there are the hand spade and the oval spade. The fourth type is the shoulder blade of the bison. Just as with the hoe, most of the spades were brought into the Rocky Mountain region from other parts of the country.

STONE BALLS

Stone balls are found in the Rocky Mountain region. They range in size from about five pounds to twenty pounds. Many so-called stone balls are just natural formations, or stones worn smooth and round by glacial action or erosion by wind, sand and water, but occasionally one is found which has been made by human hands. There was one found in a grave, the ball resting on the elbow of the skeleton.

The question that comes to mind is, "What were they used for?" There are various answers which may be given. One suggestion is that they were game balls used by the Indians to play certain types of games. This idea is probably based on the fact that many of these are about the size and shape of our bowling balls. It is sometimes believed that they were ceremonial pieces. This seems to be a general answer for the use of many artifacts for which the collector can find no other purpose.

Others believe they were a weapon, possibly suggested by the resemblance to a cannon ball, but it is very doubtful if the Indian would work a boulder to the shape of a sphere, when the original boulder would have served as well. The idea was that they could be wrapped in buckskin, used as a sling, and whirled around the head to strike an enemy. One of the most plausible theories is that they were grain or seed grinders. According to this method the grain was placed on a rock with a concave surface and then crushed and ground up as meal by rolling the ball over it. The weight of the ball

Top row—1, 2, 3, soapstone bowls. Second row—1, pestle; 2, paint bowl; 3, maul; 4, shaft straightener. Third row—1, ax; 2, stem hoe, 3, celt or tomahawk; 4, spade. Fourth row—1, chipped, double-bit ax; 2, 3, 4 and 5, polished stone axes. Collection of the late C. A. Kinsey, Belgrade, Montana.

would help in grinding the meal. Children could have used them in this manner.

These balls are not common and collectors who have them value them highly. The only problem is to tell the ones made by glacier action and erosion and the ones made by the Indian. The Indian ball is usually much rougher on the surface, probably having been made by the peck method, and is more perfectly round than the ones made by nature. See page 143.

THE CUP STONE

The cup stone is the name applied to slabs or boulders with many little indentations in them. These stones, pitted with the so-called cups, vary greatly in size. Some are cupped only on one side while others have them on both sides; the number of cups varies from two or three to over a hundred.

One authority states that they were used to hold nuts to be cracked. This removed the danger of bruising the fingers and made it possible to crack several nuts at one time.

Some believe the women used them in weaving, placing one end of the spindle in these cups. They may have been used as mortars in which meal was ground very fine, or as cups in which to mix various kinds of paint.

They may have been used to grind the ends of sticks into convex shapes, such as fire sticks for starting fires. It seems to me that we often make a mistake by stating that a certain tool was used for only one thing. It is very likely these cup stones could have been used for more than one purpose. Illustrated on page 75.

SINKERS

Sinkers are usually flat stones with notched edges. They were tied to buckskin thongs or grape vines and dragged

Top row—1, chisel; 2, war club; 3, medicine man's rattle. Second row—1, porcupine tail used as comb by Indians; 2, hoe; 3, moccasin last; 4, tomahawk. Third row—1, elk horn scraper; 2, stone ball. Fourth row—1, horse tail lash; 2, polished rose bud beads; 3, stone ring; 4, beaded Indian medicine man's bag. Moccasin last, E. C. Swallow Collection; others, Walter Jones Collection.

along the bottom of the stream to scare the fish out of shallow water so they could be caught or driven into traps prepared by the Indians. Some artifacts which we often call hammer stones could have been used for this purpose. These stones could also have been used to hold nets vertically in the water so that fish would swim into them and become entangled. They are generally found in lake regions. They are similar to artifacts known as war clubs, horse hobbles, etc., and many have been used for similar purposes. Illustration may be found on page 69.

CHAPTER 14

MISCELLANEOUS ARTIFACTS

BEADS AND WAMPUM

INDIAN beads were made of various materials such as shell, bone, pearls, stone, metals, porcupine quills, gum, wood, pottery, teeth and seeds. When they were made of metal, they were usually of gold, silver or copper. Many trade beads are found with other Indian artifacts. Columbus was probably the first to bring trade beads when he gave beads to the Indians in order to win their friendship.

The shell bead is the most common in America and was made in many shapes such as disc, tubular, barrel-shaped, and spherical. The shell was considered sacred by many tribes as it came out of the water. Beads were decorated in various ways, such as by carving, painting, inlaid work, and even by putting skins over a portion of the bead. The more workmanship on the bead, the more value was placed on it.

Where did the bead originate? Many scholars have searched for this answer but so far no general answer has been obtained. Beads have been found with all primitive people. The use among these primitive peoples seems to have been the same. They were used for adornment, medium of exchange, charms, ornamentation of articles and clothing. When they were strung, they conveyed messages and ratification of treaties.

When beads were used as a medium of exchange they were spoken of as wampum. The majority of people think of wampum as being rather large discs of shell. True, these were used to some extent, but the majority of wampum was made of shell in cylindrical shape, about one quarter of an inch long and could be used as beads or as wampum.

Collectors often examine ant hills for Indian beads. If they find them, they know that an Indian grave is in the vicinity and then are able to locate it. Several types of beads are illustrated on pages 41 and 133.

PENDANTS

Pendants were ornaments worn around the neck, as lockets are worn by civilized people. They were of all shapes and materials, and were supposed to have a charm which protected him from evil spirits, lightning and consumption. See illustrated on page 147.

THE CEREMONIAL PIECE

The ceremonial pieces were rather odd, wicked-looking pieces, many of them having deeply serrated edges, and were used in lodge or religious ceremonies. Thus, the white man can obtain little information about them.

The one illustrated on page 137 was given to me by an Indian boy. When asked about it, the boy smiled and said: "You have your lodges. We have similar gatherings. I am told that you have emblems and things you use in your ceremonies. So do we. This piece is what I'd call a ceremonial piece. You cannot tell me about your lodge, neither can I tell you about mine. I trust you will treasure and keep this piece, friend teacher."

There are various pieces known as ceremonials, and while a few are authentic, the majority of them are fakes or modern.

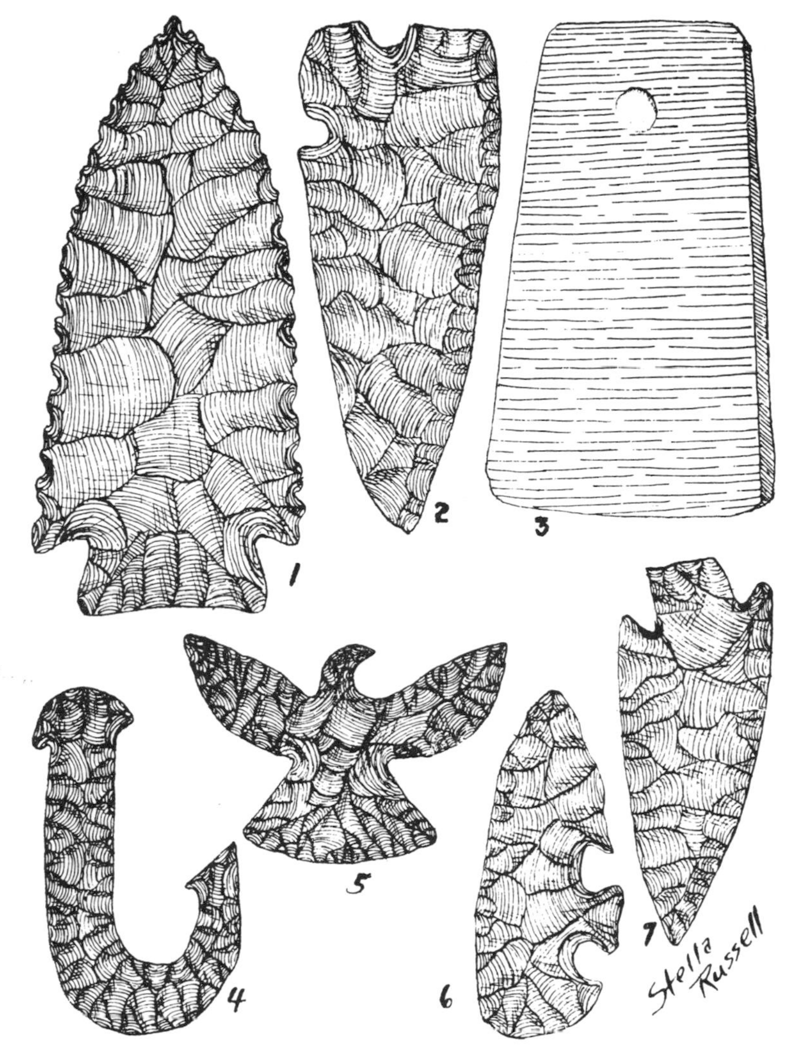

1—Serrated spear. 2—Corner tang knife. 3—Pendant. 4—Fish hook. 5—Eagle effigy. 6—Back tang knife. 7—Base tang knife. Tang knives are half size. 2 and 7, R. B. Ravenscroft Collection, Liberal Kansas; others, Walter Jones Collection.

SERRATED POINTS

The use of the majority of points and the reason for certain features about them are greatly disputed by many collectors and authorities. The serrated point is no exception to this rule. It may have been used to carry poison into the wound.

Another theory is that the serrated edge made a jagged wound which caused more suffering. This type of wound was more dangerous than the "clean cut" wound made by the average arrow point. When an arrow was shot, it traveled with great speed. Therefore, some claim that the serrated edge acted as a saw blade and penetrated deeper than a plain arrow.

Some say the arrows with large, deep serrations were fish arrows and claim they would stick into the fish better than the smooth-edged points. Others say that it was just a method of chipping. Some artifacts have very fine delicate chipping on the edge, but some Indians used a pair of stone "pliers" which left the edge of the point serrated. Some serrated edges are so delicate that they can be seen only by close scrutiny, while others are very large and deeply cut.

Regardless of the reason for the serrated edge, these artifacts are not common. A sketch appears on page 147.

THE CELT OR TOMAHAWK

The word celt seems to be in general use, but as far as I can determine there is little difference between the celt and tomahawk. *Celt* seems to be used in the East, while *tomahawk* is used in the West. Some collectors say that celt means hatchet, while others say it means chisel.

Celts are rectangular in shape, rather thin, with a sharp cutting edge. They are similar to our modern ax heads.

They were used as a fighting tool and also could be used for skinning an animal and fleshing the hide. They were not grooved as were the stone axes or mauls. Celts do not show the hard usage that the axes do.

Looking at the celt, it would seem difficult to haft. Various methods were used; I will mention the more common ones. A handle was made of wood, a notch was cut along one side of the handle and the celt was placed into the notch and lashed to the handle with buckskin thongs. Another way to attach it was to cut a hole through the handle near one end, push the smaller end of the celt through as far as it would go, then lash it tightly to the handle to hold it in place. Again, a hole was cut partly through the handle, the dull end of the celt was driven in and the sharp cutting edge allowed to protrude.

A different method was described by an old timer who told me the Indians sometimes found a sapling about the size of the handle desired. They would split it in the middle, place the celt in the cut and allow the sapling to grow around it. When the celt was firmly wedged in the young tree, they would cut off a piece of the tree. In some cases, tree gum was used to help hold the celt in place.

A few celts have been found which are sharp on both edges, similar to our double bit axes.

Various artifacts are sometimes referred to as tomahawks, but they were war clubs, not tomahawks or celts. Illustrated on page 77 and 111.

WAR CLUBS

The war club was a weapon used only in battles as the name indicates. The celt, tomahawk, ax and maul, while used in battle, were also useful in numerous other ways. War clubs were of various sizes and shapes. They ranged from heavy clubs, similar to a policeman's club, to hafted pieces of jagged stone.

One unusual type was a round ball of granite which was wrapped in buckskin and used as a sling, or lashed to a wooden handle and used as a club.

THE EFFIGY PIECE

Many of the Indians made effigy pieces. They were worn as charms or ornaments. They are seldom found in the Rocky Mountain region, though some have been found. The eagle is probably the most common style, shown in many variations of size and shape. There are also stone effigies patterned after the turtle, the lizzard, the tree, the wild goose, the snake and many others too numerous to mention. Some collectors prize them highly and others are afraid that they are fakes or modern pieces. While there are undoubtedly many fake ones, there is no question that the Indian himself made many of these stone pieces to be worn or carried as charms. See page 147 for illustrations.

TEPEE RINGS

Tepee rings were large, irregular circles made by placing rough stones side by side. The size of the circles varied from four to six paces in diameter. They were usually used as "foundations" for tents. The Indians left these stone circles when they moved from a camp site so that they or other Indians, returning to this same location might use them again.

Tepee rings and camp grounds are usually found along a river, on the shore of a lake or in a sheltered place. Year after year these places served as a camp ground, for the Indians moved about the country according to the available game supply and various seasons.

These artifacts are well arranged in geometric designs. Harold C. Towns Collection, Hillsdale, Wyoming.

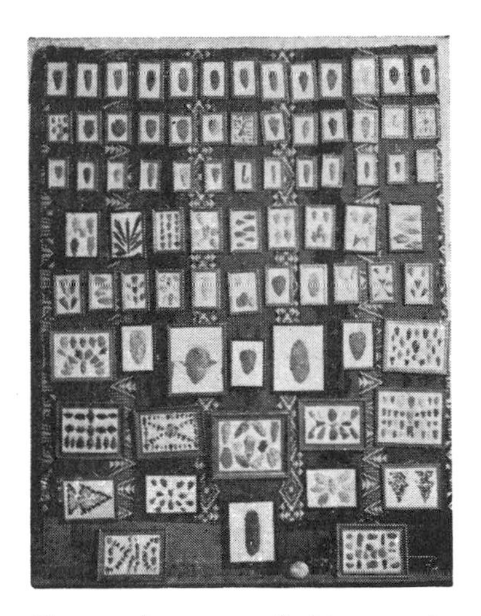

Frames hung on "white man's Indian blanket." Walter Jones Collection.

Tepee rings and fire sites mark the camp grounds. The camp fires can be located by the blackened stones and ashes. These make excellent places to search for artifacts of all kinds. Many of the artifacts which are found may be broken ones, but Indian life can be studied from these fragments. It is a pity that these camp sites cannot be preserved for study by scholars instead of being torn to pieces by vandals, curiosity seekers and would-be archaeologists. Too many of these excellent locations for studying the Indian are destroyed. The ground of the camp site should be carefully removed and the dirt screened for all artifacts.

FISH HOOKS

Fish hooks are sometimes found in the Rocky Mountain region. The majority of them are made of sharp, curved bone. They are occasionally made of stone, but the bone hook was easier to make and more effective in operation. At times, large, heavy, rather crude hooks are found; these were fastened on a long, straight pole, and then hooked under the gills of a large fish to pull him out. One is illustrated on pages 41 and 147.

PAINT BOWLS

Paint bowls were stone bowls of various shapes in which the Indian mixed his paint. They were usually very small so that they could be easily carried from place to place.

Many people ask, "Why did the Indian paint his face and body?" The generally accepted reason is that he did this so that he would look ferocious and grotesque in order to strike fear into his enemy. However, a Cheyenne Indian, Wooden Leg, said it was for an entirely different reason. He contended the Indian painted before going into battle, because, if he were killed and went to meet the "Great Spirit," he would give a better appearance. He believed the paint improved his looks and he wished to be at his best when he met the Great Spirit.

Indians sometimes painted their faces and body for protection against the wind and sun, similar to the use of face creams and lotions today, according to some authorities. Paint was also put on to designate tribes and clans. Members of some tribes used it to indicate mourning.

When the Indians were placed on reservations, they would occasionally leave the reservation to go on the war path. It is quite plausible that the Indian used paint at such times to disguise himself. Many squaw men used to go with the Indians on these raids and by using paint, it was very difficult to distinguish them from real Indians.

The colors were made from minerals, vegetables and berries. Probably the most common color was red, which was obtained from powdered iron oxide ore. Green was obtained from copper ore. Black, a color to denote death, was obtained from charcoal. Usually, the paint was mixed with the fat of animals, and then applied to the skin.

STONE RINGS

Stone rings are found in various parts of the country, but more frequently in the southwestern part of the Rocky Mountain region. The majority of them are made of lava rock; occasionally one is found which is made of granite or other material. The use or purposes? Again, the answer is problematical. The answer most frequently advanced is that they were used in games and were called game rings. The rings may have been thrown into the air and caught on sticks as they came down. Another theory is that they were thrown at pegs driven into the ground in an endeavor to make a "ringer," much in the same manner that the game of horse shoe is played today.

It is sometimes stated that they were used to weight down a net used in seining for fish. Another possible use, which seems more plausible to me, is that they were used for scraping the shafts to be used with spear and arrow points. Close examination of the "hole" of the majority of these stone "doughnuts," reveals that they are sharp and rough as a file. A shaft could be run through this hole and with friction it would work into a smooth shaft. However, like many of our modern tools, they were probably used in various ways. One mistake that many collectors make is that they consider but one use for each artifact, whereas in reality it may have had several uses.

Stone rings made of lava and porous rock are rather common, but the large ones made of granite or other hard material are quite rare. Illustrated on pages 71 and 143.

INDIAN PIPES

The white man found the Indians smoking tobacco when he discovered America. That was the first knowledge the white man had of tobacco. But odd to say, the Indian did not seem to smoke it for pleasure as we do today. While many of our people have become "chain smokers" (smoke almost continually), the Indian did not. He used it mainly in ceremonial gatherings.

The smoking of tobacco seems always to have had a prominent place in all peace treaties. When the Indians met for a peace conference, they seated themselves in a circle and remained very quiet. The chief lit the pipe, took a puff or two, then passed it around the circle, until everyone had smoked it. Then the conference began. Thus, the peace pipe of which we hear so much.

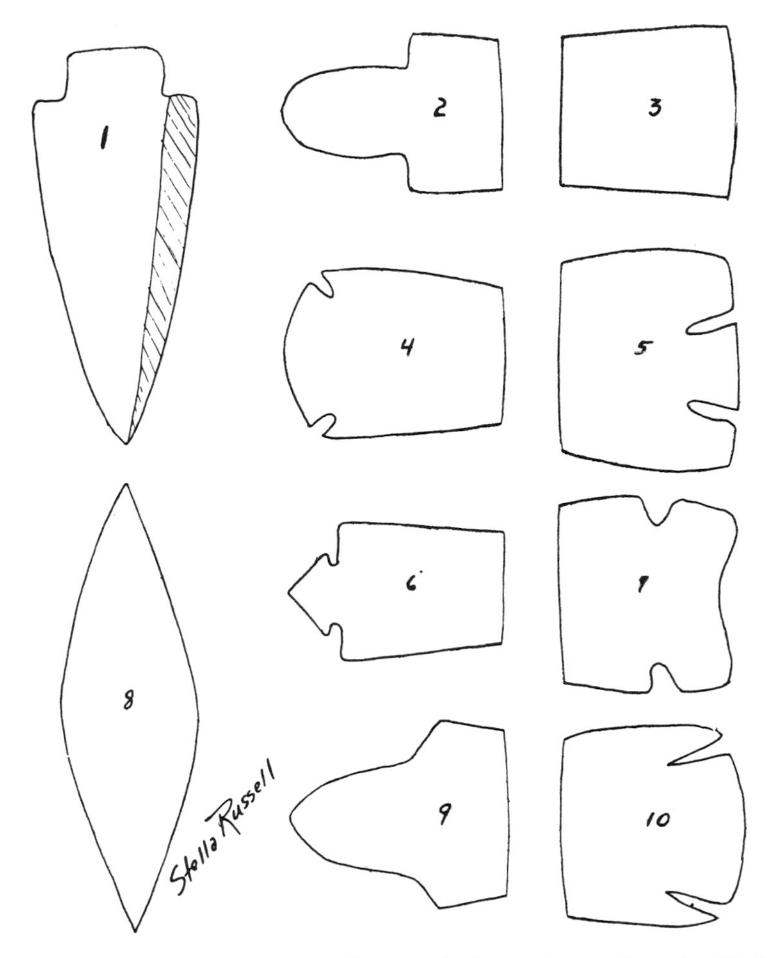

1—Beveled spear. 2—Beaver tail spear. 3—Square base, triangular blade. 4—Dove tail spear. 5—Bottom notch spear. 6—Turkey tail spear. 7—Side notch. 8—Leaf spear, pointed each end. 9—Round stemmed spear. 10—Corner notch spear.

The tobacco was sometimes adulterated with dried leaves and bark. This was probably done to save tobacco, and was considered "good medicine."

Pipes were made of various materials such as stone, clay, bone, and hard wood. The most famous quarries for pipe making material are near Pipestone, Minnesota, which contain a soft, red stone, known as catlinite. The pipes were made in various shapes and also into effigies. The most common pipe of the Rocky Mountain Region was the T-shape pipe. The famous tomahawk pipes were made by the white man and sold to the Indian. This was a two-purpose pipe which could be used as either a tomahawk or a pipe. Illustrations on page 73.

The most interesting story I ever heard concerning a pipe is the legend of the Sacred Pipe of the Arapahoes.

"A long, long time ago an Arapahoe Indian sat alone on the top of a high mountain, no other land being visible anywhere. Due to his loneliness this Indian was in tears. When the Father appeared and asked him for the cause of his tears, the Arapahoe then explained that he was alone, having no companions. The Father then summoned the dove and instructed the dove to fly over the water until he located land. At the end of three days the dove returned exhausted, telling the Father no land existed except at the point they were then on. The Father then summoned a turtle from the depths, instructed him to dive until he found earth. After several attempts the turtle came to the surface with a stone in his mouth which the Father took and, noticing under the turtle's shell a considerable amount of clay, proceeded to fashion from this a pipe and hollowed the stone which the turtle brought to the surface and used it as the bowl of the pipe. Having a slight amount left, the Father threw this into the water, but the Arapahoe, understanding the significance of this, begged the Father not to allow his people to die out,

Representative frames of the fine, large Jimmy Allen collection in Cody, Wyoming. Mr. Allen discovered and reported the now famous Jimmy Allen Yuma Site on Sagebrush Creek near Cody. These frames are picturesque in the arrangement of the various artifacts. Arrows, spears, knives, scrapers, drills, awls, tang knife and Yumas may be seen in the frames. Few collectors have done as much to preserve and gather Wyoming artifacts.

a fact which was implied by the dropping of the clay into the water. The Father, taking pity on the Arapahoe promised him that the land from which the clay had come should belong to his people, at the same time admonishing him to guard well the pipe and also promising that until the day the pipe crumbled, his race would exist. After this, the water receded and the Arapahoe found that he was left with a helpmate."

This Sacred Pipe is still in the possession of the Arapahoe tribe and is somewhere on or near the Wind River Reservation. A special custodian is responsible for its guarding. At certain times when members have reached the age necessary to be allowed to view the pipe, ceremonies consisting of fasting and prayer and lasting a week, are conducted by the tribe and the members of the tribe who are to be allowed to see the pipe. The belief of the tribe in the legend is so great that it almost amounts to worship.

GRAVE POINTS

It is against the law in many states to dig up Indian graves; it should be in all the states. But regardless of that, many people do dig up graves. They may not be any worse than the collectors who knowingly purchase articles taken from graves.

Frequently, many very fine and delicate points are found in graves. The points show that they have no use and have a new appearance. Some collectors say that the best arrow makers of the tribe made these beautiful specimens to be buried with the Indian so that he might have them to use in the happy hunting ground. Others say that they were the best points the Indian possessed, and, like his favorite horse, were buried with him.

CHAPTER 15

ARTIFACTS OF RECENT ORIGIN

THE MODERN ARTIFACT

THE majority of collectors confuse "modern" and "fake" pieces. A modern piece is an artifact made by an Indian, perhaps within the past twenty or thirty years. Collectors differ as to where the term modern begins. On the above assumption, that which is modern now will not be so a hundred years hence. Personally, I term a point modern that has been made since the period when the white man generally settled that particular locality.

The modern pieces are usually made for just one thing —to sell. I have no idea how many Indians today are turning out artifacts, for I am told that the Indians of Mexico are still making them. The modern artifacts usually show coarse workmanship; the chips are short and do not carry very far across the face of the point. However, just as the Indians today make rugs, blankets, and beadwork, they still make a few stone artifacts. There is very little of it done, as it takes time and is a tedious job. The price the Indian receives is so small that it does not pay him to make artifacts to sell.

FAKE ARTIFACTS

The fake artifact that may creep into a collection does more than any other single thing to discourage collectors. It is not only in artifact collecting that we find fakes, but in all lines of collecting, such as antiques, dishes, coins, autographs and paintings. It is doubtful if the collector of Indian artifacts is plagued with these pests and swindlers to any greater extent than collectors in general are.

How are fake artifacts made? One way is to flake them with modern tools, just as the Indian did with his crude tools. The majority of the flaking is done with steel tools. One can usually find some of the steel stain still on the piece by using a high-powered magnifying glass and checking it closely, regardless of how careful the fellow has been to remove it. The fakers usually work on soft stone or obsidian. Obsidian is used in making fake points, for it is easy to chip and makes beautiful artifacts. That is why so many collectors are not interested in obsidian artifacts. This is a pity, because obsidian artifacts are very attractive and beautiful and there are many genuine obsidian arrowheads. Many collectors question obsidian pieces which are too bright and shiny.

There are fakers who melt glass and other material and pour it into moulds. Usually these are easily detected, for they are too smooth. Normally, one could determine whether or not a piece showed age, but this is sometimes put on the point artificially by putting grease on it to give it the appearance of age. However, mechanic's soap or strong washing powder will wash off the grease and usually reveal whether or not it is a genuine piece.

One can often determine whether or not an artifact is of recent origin by rubbing the hand gently over the surface of the artifact. Recent chipping is still sharp where the chips have been removed, while the ancient piece will be dull and smooth where chips have been removed. The only place there should be any sharpness on a genuine artifact is along the edge or at the point. Years of study and close association with artifacts will give you a "beware sense" and you will come to know instinctively. It's like the glass or diamond ring, the inexperienced has difficulty in determining the genuine diamond, but the expert knows at once.

Artifacts may be divided into three classes: the ones that are genuine beyond a doubt, the ones that are questionable and the ones that are definitely fakes. A collector should not have anything to do with the two latter classes of artifacts. If there is any question about the genuineness of a point, it should never be purchased. One should obtain the full history of a piece before buying.

If you find a fellow who has a small collection, takes pride in the fact that he found every piece locally, you are usually safe in buying from him.

A law should be passed which would make it a crime to counterfeit any valuable relics such as antiques, Indian artifacts, paintings, dishes, etc. There is a heavy penalty for counterfeiting money; why not make it a severe penalty to counterfeit any other "collector's" item?

The amount of fake "stuff" on the market is not as plentiful as the average person would have you believe. If you have a good collection, others are frequently jealous and like to say "fake." Never call any collector's items "fakes" if you can avoid it. You either imply that he is "dumb" or that he is "dishonest," or both.

The best and surest way to get a collection is to go out and find it. But, if you care to purchase your artifacts your chances of being cheated are no greater in this field of collecting than in any other.

Also, do not call a piece that has been mended or rebuilt, a fake. It is no more a fake than the skeleton of a prehistoric animal which has been partially restored. If you rebuild a piece, be sure to mention this fact when showing your collection, even though it is very evident that it is restored in part. The weight, luster, and color of these points can easily be detected; even the chipping and hardness is very different from that of the genuine artifacts.

If you are careful in your selections, go slowly and use good judgment, you should have little difficulty in obtaining genuine pieces.

As a suggestion, if you find a piece you really want, and doubt its genuineness, ask for permission to send it to the Smithsonian or the curator of some large museum for their decision. Enclose return postage and a dollar or two for their effort. While it may not be necessary to enclose the money, I believe you will agree with me that it is a courteous gesture. Frequently, the owner will become indignant and refuse to allow you to check the artifact if it is a fake. Then your question is practically answered.

HOW TO MAKE ARROWHEADS

The best advice on how to make Indian arrowheads is: "Don't!" Never even try. If someone comes along and finds you endeavoring to turn out a crude arrow, the rumor will get out, "He makes his arrowheads. His collection consists mainly of fakes."

It is just as foolish as it would be to see how closely you can counterfeit money, but if it became known that you were making it, it would surely cause you a great deal of trouble. The same is true concerning the making of Indian artifacts.

Several states have tried to pass laws making it a crime to "fake" Indian artifacts, but as far as I know none has been passed. Naturally, if you made and sold them through the mails, it would be a federal offense. The only exception to this is if you are an Indian. If an Indian makes arrows and spears, the work is modern, not fake.

ACKNOWLEDGMENTS

This is the portion of my book that really deflates my ego. I suddenly realize what a flop my book would be without help, encouragement, assistance and "loans" from many people. It would be impossible for the majority of authors to really acknowledge all of the people who have helped in some way; so it is with me. Possibly it was a brief conversation, a paragraph read—maybe years ago—a picture, a drawing, a map, all of these submerged in my subconscious mind and come back to me as my own brain child that form thoughts set down on paper. I know writers who believe everything of knowledge that has already passed into the great beyond is waiting to enter some receptive mind and be placed on paper. I do not subscribe to this school of thought, but I do agree that among the "impossibilities" in the world, is a book without an error and I am sure this is one portion that if it does not contain many errors, there are probably many omissions.

I will mention friends and helpers alphabetically so that I will not have to weigh their contributions and speak of them in order of their merit. I will try to be like the old German father who used to whip each of his children every Saturday night for the times they had been bad during the week and that he hadn't caught them. "Dey put nothing over on dis father!"

And so, "Dey put nothing over on dis author!" I thank them, one and all.

Jimmy Allen of Cody discovered the Cody site and helped work on the *dig*. He furnished me much information on how this discovery was made and had pictures of the Yumas found there. The late Perry Anderson, who found the original Yuma collection, told me many interesting facts about the Yuma, "Buck" Burshears, La Junta, Colorado, organized the world famous Koshare Indians and gave me information on the Indian customs, dances and artifacts in general. Robert B. David, a Wyoming historian, was very helpful in his suggestions on Indian lore and history. Vernon Drake, Sterling, Kansas, answered questions about Kansas artifacts.

Mr. and Mrs. Luther Eckles, San Diego, California, told me about the Pinto Basin Point and gave me specimens to picture and draw. H. E. Fronville, dealer and collector of Watseka, Illinois, furnished me with pictures of his collection and checked over my material to note omissions. M. R. Harrington, curator of the Southwest Museum, Los Angeles, sent pictures and information about the Lake Mohave, Silver Lake and Gypsum Cave points. Dr. Frank C. Hibben, University of New Mexico, sent me most of my information on the Sandia.

Malcolm W. Hill of Alexandria, Virginia, has helped me not only with this third printing, but the other two, by furnishing much information on the hafting of Indian stone tools and mending broken artifacts. Mr. Hill has written many fine articles on the subject of Indian relics and he sent me numerous manuscripts with permission to use any or all of his material. It is doubtful if any living man today knows as much about the methods of hafting stone tools as Mr. Hill. I certainly consider Mr. Hill an authority on this subject and well informed on the Indian in general. My only regret is that I could not include more of his original material.

Dr. Glenn L. Jepsen, Professor of Vertebrate Paleontology, Princeton University, worked on the Yuma site at Cody, Wyoming. He and his associates unearthed much valuable information on Yuma man's artifacts. Walter Jones of Casper, permitted me to photograph many of his fine artifacts. Rev. Sterling P. Martz, of Shamokin, Pennsylvania sent me pictures of his Yumas and Folsoms.

The late Ed McQuinn, of Casper, did more than any other man to influence and mold my ideas on quality and not quantity in artifacts. "No price is too high to pay for a 'super' artifact; any price is too high for a cull." "Suspicion the parentage of every specimen until it is proved authentic." Ed is gone but not forgotten. Vernon Mokler, Casper, told me many of his ideas and theories on Wyoming Indians and artifacts.

Mr. and Mrs. M. P. Mosbrucker, Mandan, North Dakota, furnished all of the information on the Mandan Indians which appears in the book. They sent me many pictures and even sent me a large number of valuable Mandan artifacts to photograph and draw. It is one of the few times a collector has trusted me enough to send me his choice artifacts to study and picture. I consider both Mr. and Mrs. Mosbrucker authorities on the Mandan Indians. I doubt if any other living persons have made such an extensive and intensive study of the Mandan Indians and are so willing to share that knowledge.

Mr. R. B. Ravenscroft of Liberal, Kansas, sent me pictures of his corner tang knife collection. Dr. E. B. Renaud, and I have included it in this volume. Mr. Charles Rhoton, Jr., of Keyes, Oklahoma, has assisted me in obtaining names and addresses of collectors. Mr. Rhoton takes pride in his Yumas.

Dr. Frank H. H. Roberts, Jr., of the Smithsonian Institute, sent me pictures of the Agate Basin points. He also answered many perplexing questions on numerous artifacts. Dr. Roberts is undoubtedly one of the foremost living authorities on Indian artifacts and has been helpful in all three printings of INDIAN ARTIFACTS. Tom Sandison, Casper, photographed his very fine corner tang knife, probably the finest ever found, so that it could be included in my book. E. B. Sayles, curator of the Arizona Museum, Tucson, furnished me with pictures and information on the Hohokam points. Mack Schumm, Circleville, Ohio, sent me pictures and information on the fractured base points and assisted in gathering the names of many collectors for my files.

Mr. B. W. Stephens, as librarian for the Central States Archaeological Society, 815 Broadway, Quincy, Illinois, granted me permission to use many of the fine cuts which appear regularly in the very outstanding magazine, "Central States Archaeological Journal." I consider these cuts some of the finest illustrations in my book. It was certainly a big help to my book to have this material. Mr. E. C. Swallow, Casper, has an outstanding collection of artifacts and furnished me with specimens to photograph. He has always extended a helping hand.

Willis G. Tilton, 1615 West 21st St., Topeka, Kansas, is a collector and dealer and was helpful in giving suggestions about the book, as to name, composition, etc. Dr. T. Hugh Young, Nashville, Tennessee, invited me to see his outstanding museum and answered many questions concerning his "collection of collections." To the best of my knowledge, he has *the* outstanding private museum of the country. Mr. Edward Zimmerman, dealer and collector of 102 Long Street, Bonne Terre, Missouri, sent me a picture of his collection and tracings of artifacts I had omitted in my first two printings. He also furnished me with much information on Missouri artifacts.

Last of all, but by no means least, I acknowledge the help of my wife Stella who has made all of the drawings, photographed many of the artifacts, typed and corrected all of the manuscript, keeps the books and wraps and sends out all of the orders.

And now let me end by expressing my thanks and appreciation for all of the help, however trivial, from the many wonderful collectors from coast to coast, somewhere in between A and Z, that I am unable to mention personally in this chapter; they too have my deepest gratitude.

INDEX OF ARTIFACTS